PRIORITIES
—— FOR THE ——
CHURCH

PRIORITIES
—— FOR THE ——
CHURCH

REDISCOVERING LEADERSHIP AND VISION IN THE CHURCH

DONALD MACLEOD

CHRISTIAN FOCUS PUBLICATIONS

Donald Macleod is Principal of the Free Church of Scotland College in Edinburgh, Scotland, where he also lectures in Systematic Theology. He has written several books for Christian Focus. He is regularly called on to present the Christian viewpoint on current issues on radio and television, and frequently writes newspaper articles. His other books include:-

Shared Life - The Trinity and the Fellowship of God's People
ISBN 1 85792 128 3
From Glory to Golgotha - Controversial Issues in the Life of Christ
ISBN 1 85792 718 4
Rome and Canterbury - A View from Geneva
ISBN 0 906 73188 7
The Spirit of Promise - The Truth about the Holy Spirit
ISBN 0 906 73148 8
Behold Your God
ISBN 1 87167 650 9
And in the *Mentor* Imprint
Jesus Is Lord - Christology, Yesterday and Today
ISBN 1 85792 485 1
A Faith to Live By - Understanding Christian Doctrine
ISBN 1 85792 428 2

© Donald Macleod
ISBN 1 85792 693 5

Published in 2003
by Christian Focus Publications,
Geanies House, Fearn, Ross-shire
IV20 1TW, Great Britain

www.christianfocus.com

Cover design by Alister Macinnes

CONTENTS

INTRODUCTION

This is a short book, but it was long in the making. All but one of the chapters originally appeared in the *Monthly Record* during my time as editor (1978–1991). The remaining article, 'The Basis of Christian Unity,' was first published in *Evangel*, journal of Rutherford House, Edinburgh.

Why re-publish them now? My only defence is that whatever the inadequacies of the answers, the questions these articles address are as urgent today as they were twenty years ago. Preaching is at a discount. Ministers are confused as to their role. Ecumenical advance is blocked by the non-negotiable assumptions of those who masquerade as the most enthusiastic advocates of Christian unity. And Christianity remains discredited by lamentable discord and division.

All these issues have followed us into the new millennium. Eventually, one hopes, they will command the rigorous attention of the great scholars of the church. In the meantime, the merely journalistic contributions which make up this book may help to focus Christian minds and stimulate Christian thought.

As ever, I am grateful to Christian Focus Publications, and particularly to the Editor, Malcolm Maclean, for their patience, courtesy and expertise.

1

THE
MINISTRY
TODAY

There is never an appropriate time to write about the ministry. Those still actively engaged in it are too closely involved and too inclined to major on what they themselves do best. Those who have left (especially to work in theological colleges) live in ivory towers, out of touch with reality. But someone must talk about it.

Ministers today, in all denominations, face a role-crisis. What is expected of them? Are these expectations biblical? And to what extent can they be fulfilled?

General principles
Let's begin with two general principles.

First of all, the minister must be a human being. The point is not quite as obvious as it seems. 'One of my brothers,' said an American wag, 'is a minister. The other is a human being.' It is something we easily lose. Indeed, some of us lose it deliberately, as if we had to choose between ministry and humanity. We don't dress like humans. We don't speak like humans (especially when we're preaching). We don't have to worry about mortgages and redundancy; or about budgetary constraints and efficiency studies. We feel unable to admit weakness, fallibility or temptation. We cannot have ordinary social lives ('Don't have friends in the congregation!' used to be very common, and very bad, advice).

The only remedy is to refuse to be put into this mould. Ordination should not change us overnight. We should keep our old friends, guard against humbug and pretentiousness, admit our own limitations, ask for help, accept help and give thanks for help. We should meet the rest of the congregation in as many ordinary situations as possible and expect no more deference from them than we are prepared to extend in return. As far as possible we should live as they live, sharing their fears and frustrations.

This is not some concession to a passing fad. It is absolutely imperative. Without humanity we are useless. We cannot even pray for our people unless we feel with them. The Lord Himself, after all, had to be a compassionate and faithful High Priest; and He could only be such by being touched with the feeling of our infirmities.

Secondly, if we may be forgiven a moment of jargon, all ministry must be contextualised. General principles there may be, but they have to be applied in very particular situations. Our minds may be steeped in the theological literature of the seventeenth or the nineteenth century, but we are ministering in the twenty-first. Our roots may be in the Highlands, our ministry in the Lowlands. Our predilection may be for rural life, our vocation in the city. Our personal Bible may be the NIV., that of our people the KJV. All such details demand adjustment, and maybe even sacrifice, on our part. The strange thing is that many men who would be perfectly prepared to contextualize if sent to Indonesia, are often reluctant to do so when sent to Airdrie or Achiltibuie. Yet the principle, again, is a fundamental one. We have to be all things to all men. Part of what it means to be called to the ministry is to be spiritually sensitive, able to read situations and to work out exactly what is called for. Are we in the Highlands or in the Lowlands? Are we facing intellectuals or artisans, spiritual babes or spiritual giants, a church with long traditions or a church with none? We will only make such judgments, of course, if we accept the need to distinguish between the gospel and our cultural baggage. What belongs to the gospel cannot be abandoned. What is purely cultural can. Justification by faith is an essential in every church. Having preparatory services prior to Communion is not.

The ministry of the Word

But what are our specific expectations?

Most obviously that the minister will be a preacher and teacher. It has to be conceded at once that he is not the only one charged with such responsibilities and should not feel threatened or resentful when other members of the congregation engage in various forms of teaching. All elders, for example, are expected to be 'apt to teach'. Parents are expected to instruct their children, older women to teach younger women and all of us to give a good account of our faith. And it would be a sad day if our churches no longer had their Priscillas and Aquilas to look after promising young converts. In short, all Christians have a teaching ministry. This was a marked feature of the life of the early church: so much so in fact that one of the Fathers commented, 'In the beginning all taught and all baptised.'

What distinguishes the minister is that preaching and teaching is his life's work: his major, and indispensable, contribution to the church. Others may do it occasionally: he labours at it. He has, as we shall see, other tasks as well. But these are things he shares with others. What the church needs from him is preaching. If he doesn't supply it the whole body suffers; and it is no compensation that he is a nice man, a good visitor, or an expert at repairing drains or making sandwiches.

How can we hope to do it well?

First, by making it our priority. It's what ministers exist for: what they're supposed to give their best strength to. Being a preacher is not simply an activity. It's a lifestyle. It shapes our perception of everything that goes on around us. The outstanding example of this is the Lord Himself. Birds and lilies, sowing and harvesting, fishing and commerce, shepherding, vine-dressing and children playing: all were grist to the mill of his teaching and preaching. A good preacher never switches off.

Secondly, by making sure that we spend every forenoon in our studies. Sadly, things are such in the churches today that men feel ashamed if found with a book. The moment we sit in our studies the Devil brings to mind the people we haven't visited, the letters we haven't written and the thing we meant to discuss with the Clerk of the Deacons' Court. There is only one answer: a *cordon sanitaire* around the hours from nine to one. They should be absolutely sacred. There is no excuse for a minister being seen out of doors before lunchtime. Apart from the occasional funeral, every morning is his own. More precisely, it is his congregation's: to be spent for them in the closet, engaged in prayer and in study of theWord of God. It should not even be a time of sermon preparation. It should be a time of self-preparation: feeding our souls, filling our minds and stimulating our mental and spiritual processes. During these times the preacher communes with God, pores over the word and enjoys the fellowship of the great master-preachers and master-theologians of all ages. Having spent the week in God's market, there is some hope that he can then provide his people with the feast they deserve.

There is nothing at all unrealistic about this. A preacher who has no time for study is like a professional footballer who has no time for training. Certainly the pressure of work is no excuse. C. H. Spurgeon found (or made) time in an incredibly busy life to read six books a week. Daniel Rowland, the outstanding preacher of the Methodist revival in Wales, was an obsessive student: 'When at home,' wrote his biographer, 'he spent most of his time in his study, and it was almost impossible to get him out of it, according to the testimony of his daughter. Early in 1738 Howell Harris heard that Rowland was studying so hard that "he lost his hair and sleep".' Such men are surely a rebuke to us. But the reason for their commitment to study was simple: preaching mattered more to them than anything else in the world.

Which brings us to the third thing: effective preaching depends on our being obsessed with our craft. It is fashionable today to despise homiletics. The contempt is difficult to understand. Paul, after all, preached in weakness and fear and much trembling. He was afraid of himself. Was he doing it right? Was the content right? Was the presentation right? These questions obsess all preachers; and they will seek help wherever it can be found. They will observe others at work. They will read the great preachers of the past (and of the present). They will read their biographies, looking for the secret of their power. And they will read every book on homiletics they can lay hands on: Shedd, Dabney, Alexander, Brooks, Spurgeon, Blaikie, Beecher, Blackie, Stalker, Black, Stewart, Mackenzie, Lloyd-Jones and everyone else.

Fourthly, the preacher must be fully involved with his people. His responsibility, after all, is to take the Word to the world; and to do that he must know both. He gets to know the Word in his study. He can get to know his people only by meeting them: as far as possible, on their terms. Then his preaching will be truly pastoral, aimed, not at his fellow theologians, nor at the Christians he knew in his youth, nor at the church of the past, but at the people actually sitting in front of him. He will know their problems, fears and hang-ups; their lack of assurance; their difficulties at work; their doubts; their ethical dilemmas; their backslidings. He will know what they're interested in; what they read; what they watch on television; and what they're taking in of what they hear on Sundays. He will know the spiritual risks they face. And he will choose his texts accordingly, earthing his preaching in the needs of real people. He will work out not simply what the text means in a historico-grammatical sense but what it's saying here and now to his people. He will never be content simply to explain it. He will apply it; and he will apply it to those sitting in front of him.

Fifthly, the minister must realise that there are more ways of preaching and teaching than standing in a pulpit delivering sustained, logical, uninterrupted discourses. These are, obviously, enormously important. There is abundant biblical precedent for them and God has blessed them mightily. In fact, as the examples of Edwards, Whitefield, Rowland, MacDonald and many others show, this is what He has normally used to bring revival to His church. But it is not the only way. Preaching does not necessarily presuppose a large audience. When Philip spoke to the Ethiopian Chancellor in a one-to-one situation, that was preaching. In the old days in Scotland, ministers practised catechizing, which obviously involved a high degree of audience participation. Men like Hog of Kiltearn in Scotland and Daniel Rowland in Wales made regular use of Fellowship Meetings. The need today is even more pressing. Ministers must get down from their pulpits to listen to their people, answer their questions, meet their objections and hear their suggestions. And, of course, to ask their own questions. Apart from all else, the exercise will give us some indication of our own effectiveness. It can be a salutary experience after many years in a congregation to hear people speak in a way that betrays all too clearly that they still haven't grasped the most fundamental principles of Christianity. The test then is whether we blame the people for their obtuseness or ourselves for our inadequacy as preachers.

Counselling

But preaching is not the only thing. The minister is also a counsellor, expected to encourage, admonish and to give advice on a wide range of behavioural and emotional problems. As such problems multiply so the pressure for help becomes greater; and since such a ministry seems, at least on the face of things, rewarding and meaningful, many 'feel this is what they should be doing'. This creates its own dangers, not least for the concept of the ministry itself. In America, particularly, many have abandoned a ministry of the word for a ministry of counselling. This leads, in turn, to pressure for changes in ministerial training. The traditional curriculum, with its emphasis on biblical and theological studies, prepared men to preach. Now there is an increasing demand for men trained to counsel and for a curriculum weighted in favour of psychology, sociology and related disciplines.

How should we react? By keeping a sense of biblical proportion. This involves several factors.

First, we have to recognise that many Christians urgently need counselling. They are discouraged, depressed, backslidden, living in sin, missing from church meetings, dabbling in drink, indulging in sinful relationships, worldly. They are failing as husbands and wives, as parents and children. They are having difficulties at work. They are ridden with doubt. Such problems are too often ignored, sometimes because too many people (including the minister) feel, 'It's none of my business!', sometimes because people feel helpless and sometimes because people feel they would be compromised by talking to the disgraced. Our glaring failure in this area is one of the main reasons for leakage from the church in recent years.

Secondly, the minister was never meant to bear the whole burden of pastoral ministry on his own. Apart from all else, it is physically impossible. Counselling is a labour-intensive activity. A man who makes himself available day and night to half-a-dozen people with serious behavioural problems will soon find that he has little time for sleep and none at all for sermon preparation. The pattern God has established in His word is that the pastoral burden is to be shared. All elders are pastors, charged with oversight and endowed with the gifts needed to encourage and admonish their flocks. But the responsibility doesn't end even with the elders. All Christians have pastoral responsibilities. Paul makes this clear in 1 Thessalonians 5:14: 'We beseech you, brethren, warn those that are unruly, comfort the feeble-minded, support the weak.' The burden does not fall on the office-bearers: it falls on the brethren (and, of course, on the sisters as well). Many problems escalate only because those close to them choose to ignore them. If all of us, not least the women of the church, accepted our pastoral responsibilities, things would be much different. This is no mandate for inquisitorial prying and meddling or for gratuitous invasion of other people's lives. Effective counselling has to be mutual; and it has to be conducted within a framework of meekness and respect. But there is no doubt that so far as the Bible is concerned every woman is her sister's keeper.

Thirdly, the minister cannot shirk his own counselling role. He is a pastor as well as a preacher. In one way or another he will learn about problems he has no right to pass on to others. He must deal with them himself. In fact, if he is as accessible to his people as he should be, they will make their way to him with their problems, as a matter of course: and they should be able to do so in absolute confidence.

All of which brings us back to the matter of training. In the last analysis, Christian counselling is neither an art nor a profession but a charisma: a spiritual gift. The Christian who engages in it relies mainly on three things: the teaching of scripture, the ministry of the Spirit and the Christian prudence acquired through his own experience. It is the application of these resources that gives what he does its distinctive character as Christian counselling. But this does not preclude training. All ministers need to be able to detect the symptoms of, for example, alcoholism and depression. All should be able to relate to disturbed people in one-to-one situations. And all should know when they are out of their depth and need to call in specialist help. There is no point at which such training ceases. It is an ongoing thing and, once the foundation is laid, almost entirely a matter of self-help. Just as the minister will read every book on preaching so he will read whatever he can lay hands on relating to counselling. Why? Because he counsels as he preaches: in fear and trembling.

Leadership

Besides being preacher and counsellor the minister is also a leader. He is not alone in this. The elders are also leaders. But so long as the minister is the only specifically trained, paid, full-time worker in the congregation the main responsibility will fall on him.

Leadership in this context means three things.

First, vision. Obviously, such a vision will have to be derived from the Bible, but each of us will have to work out what that means for his own situation. For ourself, it means a congregation which simultaneously reaches out to the wider community and is prepared to welcome all Christians simply on the basis that they are Christians. This demands that we transcend race and culture, disregard minor theological differences, major on the core doctrines of Christianity and practise the principle of Christian liberty in a way that allows God's people to be themselves. The practical test of such a congregation would be that every member could confidently take friends (converted and unconverted, rich and poor, learned and unlearned, black and white) along to the services.

Secondly, leadership involves expectations. We are bedevilled today by the wrong kind of Calvinism: one which accepts declining congregations as some inevitable consequence of predestination. Such expectations tend to be self-fulfilling. What of the great multitude which no man can number? What of the sustained New Testament emphasis on growth? What of the promise that God's word will not return to Him useless? What of the great pattern established in Acts: as men preached, God added to the church? These should be our attitudes. If we bring up our children in the knowledge of the Lord they will remain on His side; and if we nurture our congregations as we ought they will grow. If they don't grow, there is something wrong and we should be crying to God, 'Lord, how long?'

Thirdly, the leader is an enabler. He gets things done. How? Above all, by making sure that he doesn't try to do everything himself. The New Testament insists on body-ministry. Every member has a gift. Every member is baptised in the Spirit. Every member has a ministry. In fact the Body will function properly only if every component is working properly. Unfortunately, some members think they can't work. Others think they aren't allowed to work. Others don't want to work. And a few think they should do all the work. Get them all working! No one doing everything! No one doing nothing! Each making his own contribution, all teaching, all admonishing, all encouraging, all praying, all expectant. Some have precious personal skills as builders, businessmen, social workers, doctors or teachers. These are priceless resources. Use them! Consult them! Give them responsibility! Some are marvellous at bringing others to church, others marvellous at welcoming them. Thank God for them! And thank them, too! Some have heads full of ideas. Others are capable of endless hours of drudgery. Mobilise them, integrate them, use them, so that the whole body vibrates with life.

Problems?

Finally, problems. What is the main problem facing ministers today? Almost certainly, discouragement. Much of this is circumstantial. It is not an easy day to be a minister. But some of it, sadly, arises from within the church itself, frequently, indeed, from its very leadership. The minister is often under pressure to believe that his main gift, preaching, is no longer what the church needs. He must spend more time out and about! And then, when, as is inevitable, his preaching suffers, he is criticised for his preaching! There even seems to be a resentment in some quarters of preaching itself and a growing demand that it be replaced by some form of dialogue. There is no doubt that many earnest, talented and dedicated men are demoralised and dispirited. It is no fun having to face, every Sunday, instant postmortems of one's preaching; or to be in situations where, as one remarked to me recently, 'Whatever I do, it's wrong!' Few of these men are despots. Few regard themselves as above criticism. A word of encouragement might transform their ministry.

2

THE CALL
TO THE
MINISTRY

The myths which circulate with regard to the call to the ministry are legion. The most common, probably, is that such a call is a matter of special revelation. Men observe that prophets and apostles were directly commissioned by God and expect the experience of pastors to be similar. This is to forget, however, the uniqueness of the prophetic and apostolic offices. These men were the organs of special revelation, charged with laying the foundation of the church and endowed with infallible authority and plenipotentiary power. Ministers stand in a different succession, and Charles Bridges is surely correct when he writes: 'Having no extraordinary commission we do not expect an immediate and extraordinary call.' Basically, our vocation comes through providential guidance, biblical teaching and personal reflection and prayer.

Not if you can help it
Equally misleading is the familiar advice, 'Do not enter the ministry if you can help it.' Not even the fact that it is warmly endorsed by C.H. Spurgeon can redeem this principle from the charge of absurdity. This is probably why even its most ardent advocates do not apply it consistently. We do not, for example, apply it to elders and deacons. How many office-bearers would we have if every person elected delayed acceptance until God made it impossible for him to resist? Nor do we apply it to the problems of guidance in general, arguing that the only way to be sure of God's will is to resist it, confident that if something really is His will He will eventually simply force it on us. That, surely, would be to tempt the Lord our God.

In actual fact, it is perfectly possible to disobey a call to the ministry, due to fear or timidity or the pressure of other ambitions or the constraints of relatives or a mistaken waiting for blinding, visionary light or even a false modesty.

Too much is made of the reluctance of men like Moses and Jonah. Jonah was blatantly guilty of fleeing from a divine vocation and the Bible explicitly records God's disapproval of Moses' excuses: 'the anger of the Lord was kindled against Moses.' That is a high price to pay for a reputation for humility. There is a very real possibility of divine chastening for those who, in the face of divine preparation and endowment refuse to make themselves available for the ministry of the church. 'To intrude into a pulpit without a call is doubtless a sin,' wrote Robert Dabney; 'But to stay out of the pulpit when called to enter it is also a sin, a sin which can only proceed from evil motives and which must naturally result in the damnation of souls which should have been saved through the disobedient Christian's preaching, but were not, and which must bring him under the frown and chastisement of an offended Saviour.'

The leadings of providence

Another area where we can fall into serious misunderstanding is in connection with 'the leadings of providence'. These do, of course, have their own importance. If a man has no opportunity for securing basic education or suffers from chronic ill-health or has a serious speech-impediment, then it is fairly obvious that God never intended him for the Christian ministry.

Yet providence is a far from infallible guide. When Jonah was fleeing from God's will everything at first went splendidly and he might easily have argued that 'doors opened in a remarkable way'. It may indeed often happen that those whom God never called have an easy passage through the years of formal training and at the end of these have no difficulty in finding a settlement. This is only to apply, in the context of the ministry, what is often true of the ungodly in other connections: 'They are not in trouble as other men' (Ps. 73:5). On the other hand, those who are truly called may have to face many difficulties both during the years of training and in the actual work itself. Remember, for example, Paul's experience as described in 2 Corinthians 11:23ff: labour, stripes, imprisonments, rods, stonings, shipwrecks, perils, robbers, false brethren, weariness, pain, hunger, thirst, cold and nakedness, 'besides that which cometh on me daily, the cares of all the churches'. Had Paul followed 'the leadings of providence' he would surely have concluded that he was never meant to be a missionary.

Other men in the later history of the church have faced similar trials. Brainerd, Whitefield and McCheyne served through appalling ill-health; Calvin, in Geneva, faced many years of internal friction and opposition; Thomas Boston 'passed two years and three months in the character of a probationer', waiting for a congregation to give him a call. 'These years,' he wrote afterwards, 'brought in continued scenes of trial to me; being, through the mercy of God, generally acceptable to the people; but could never call into the good graces of those who had the stroke in the settling of parishes.' Even after his ordination he had to be content with the relative obscurity of two very small country parishes, Simprin and Ettrick; to say nothing of the charges of doctrinal error brought against him during the Marrow controversy. The case of John Brown of Haddington is equally interesting. He had to overcome almost hopeless educational disadvantages and then suffered the mortification of being accused of witchcraft because his progress was so remarkable.

These experiences should remind us of the need to keep a sense of proportion with regard to difficulties, discouragement, closed doors and 'impossibilities'. Sometimes, maybe, these things are meant for our guidance. But just as often, they are trials of our faith or messengers of Satan to buffet us or part of our ministerial preparation, equipping us to comfort others with the comfort God gives to ourselves. Doors will often open for the false prophet and just as often appear to close for the true one.

An irrepressible conviction

There is a fourth myth at the opposite extreme: that an irrepressible conviction of our own vocation is tantamount to a divine call. Usually, such a conviction is traced to a mystical or transcendental experience, a voice or a vision giving a compelling inner certainty.

The trouble with this is that such experiences are authoritative only for the person who has them. They have no value for others and they certainly do not warrant the church ordaining a man without carefully enquiring whether he possesses the spiritual gifts and the personal character which the Bible says are essential in a pastor. Sometimes, a very cursory examination will make plain that the applicant is deluded. He turns out to be feeble-minded or spiritually proud or censorious and autocratic or even heretical. None of these defects, apparently, is sufficient to prevent a man feeling convinced he is called to the ministry. But all of them, individually or in any possible combination, are quite sufficient to entitle the church to disagree with him.

In some other instances, applications from such a source are purely tentative and exploratory. The applicant regards his own view of his calling as final and he feels no need to submit it to the church for ratification. If one denomination does not recognise him, he will cheerfully go to another; and should none recognise him, he is quite prepared to found his own, happy so long as he can hear the sound of his own voice and unperturbed by the fact that he has excommunicated Christendom.

All interviews with candidates for the ministry should therefore contain the question: What will you do if we refuse your application? and if they are not prepared to listen to the judgment of the church, we should treat them as heathens and publicans (Matt. 18:17).

Not a call to evangelism

One further point deserves a brief mention: Men are constantly confusing the call to the ministry with the call to evangelism. It is assumed that the aim of the office is the conversion of sinners, that the basic requirement is the ability to preach to the unsaved and the unchurched, and that the final seal of divine approval will be 'souls for our hire'.

In the New Testament, however, the work of the pastor is basically quite distinct from that of the evangelist. The pastor is the overseer and teacher of a settled congregation, ministering primarily to people who know the Lord. This does not mean that he has no evangelistic function. He knows that among his regular hearers there are some who are not Christians. He is also concerned for the children of believers; and he is always conscious of the possibility of strangers dropping in to the services. But his basic ministry is to feed the flock, and if he spends his life trying to convert the converted and to drum the most elementary doctrines into his people as if they never could move on to solid food, the result will be zero growth in the life of his congregation. Conversely, anyone who can really evangelise is wasting his time in the pastorate. He should be in the spiritual wastelands bringing Christ to the ignorant and uninitiated.

Is it not possible that much of the neurosis in the ministry is due to this confusion? Men are being judged – and are judging themselves – by the wrong criteria. The pastor is not expected to be a Whitefield through whom multitudes are added to the church daily. He is the shepherd of a gathered and settled flock, concerned with the spiritual, qualitative growth of individuals and congregations. The criterion by which he should be judged is not the annual rate of conversions but the progress of his congregation in doctrine, in holiness, in brotherly love and in missionary and evangelistic zeal. The gifts that constitute his calling are not those indispensable to an itinerant, frontier evangelist, but those that will enable him, week after inexorable week, to feed the church over which God has made him an overseer.

What does the Bible teach?

The summary answer is that the call to the ministry consists of three things: a God-given desire to engage in the Word; God's bestowal of the necessary gifts; and God's leading the church to ordain the individual to a particular congregation.

Normally, when God calls to the ministry he implants a desire for the work. Paul refers to this in 1 Timothy 3:1: 'If a man desires the office of a bishop he desires a good work.' Each of the verbs used indicates *strong desire*. In fact, the second one (*epithumei*) is used in Galatians 5:17 to indicate the urgency with which the flesh lusts against the Spirit. Spurgeon is justified, therefore, in saying that 'the first sign of the heavenly call is an intense, all-absorbing desire for the work. In order to a true call to the ministry there must be an irresistible, overwhelming craving and raging thirst for telling to others what God has done to our own souls.'

Two cautions are necessary, however.

First, the absence of desire is not in itself decisive. Some men are truly called who, to begin with, shrink back with horror from the very idea. Sometimes, in fact, the call of the church has come to men like a bolt out of the blue. The classic instance of this is John Knox, who at first resisted all exhortations to preach in public, arguing that he did not consider himself to have a call. Without his knowledge, however, the garrison at St. Andrews resolved that a call should be given to him publicly. A day was fixed for this purpose and after a sermon on the election of ministers, John Rough, chaplain to the garrison, suddenly turned to Knox and addressed him as follows: 'In the name of God and of His Son, Jesus Christ, and in the name of all that presently call upon you by my mouth, I charge you that you refuse not this holy vocation, but as you tender the glory of God, the increase of Christ's kingdom, the edification of your brethren and the comfort of me, whom you understand well enough to be oppressed by the multitude of labours, that you take the public office and charge of preaching even as you look to avoid God's heavy displeasure, and desire that He shall multiply His graces unto you.' The congregation there and then publicly endorsed Rough's charge. Knox, says McCrie, made an ineffectual attempt to address the assembly but found the whole situation overwhelming, rushed out and shut himself in his room, 'his countenance and behaviour, from that day till the day that he was compelled to present himself in the public place of preaching sufficiently declaring the grief and trouble of his heart'.

The second and opposite caution is that the presence of the desire, however ardent, is not in itself an infallible sign of a call to the ministry. The desire itself must be scrutinised.

For example, what motive lies behind it? Why does a man desire to be a minister? It may be that he desires the prestige that goes along with it; or because it affords a high measure of security and abundant opportunity for seclusion and study; or because it gives us something to be lords over; or even because it affords a wide and attractive variety of job-experiences – public speaking, counselling, administration, politicking. These are very real dangers and even the best-intentioned can hardly give a confident answer to the question: 'Are not zeal for the honour of God, love to Jesus Christ and desire of saving souls, your great motives and chief inducements to enter into the function of the holy ministry, and not worldly designs and interests?'

It is also important to be sure that the desire is realistic. Sometimes a yearning for the ministry is naïve and visionary. Where there is a true vocation the desire is directed to the work as defined in Scripture – a labour (1 Tim. 3:1) and a hardship (2 Tim. 2:3). The problems are legion: the sheer number of services, the mental burden of incessant sermon preparation, the unending routine of visits, the encroachment of one's work into family life, the loneliness of pastors in isolated situations and the humiliations incidental to living in a tied house. Added to this is the problem of constant opposition: the disaffected in one's own congregation, the schemers in ecclesiastical politics and, above all, the ceaseless activities of false teachers. One learns that protestations of love and loyalty cannot be taken at face-value; one faces the heartbreak of backsliding among one's own people; and, occasionally, the tragedy of apostasy on the part of those from whom much was expected.

Any realistic desire for the ministry must be aware of these aspects of the work; and yet be prepared in God's strength to face them and even to count it a privilege to endure them.

Gifts

Where God gives the desire He will also confer the necessary gifts. The reference, of course, is to *charismata* – to spiritual gifts – not to educational attainments or business acumen or professional experience. These may have their own value. But from a theological point of view the indispensable pre-requisite for the ministry is the possession of God-given and God-sustained charismata.

God confers these gifts at three different levels.

First, at the level of leadership. Pastors (including what we call *ruling elders*) are *over* the church of God (1 Thess. 5:12). They must, therefore, have the gift of government (1 Cor. 12:28), including such qualities as initiative, courage, vigour, independence of spirit, dynamism, imagination and wisdom. It is absurd to move a man from the back seat of a church to the pulpit and expect the transition to work wonders. The proper candidates for ordination are those who have been active in bringing outsiders to church, distributing tracts, volunteering for mundane and menial tasks, offering their homes for fellowship and generating interest in Bible-study and evangelism.

Secondly, the pastor requires counselling gifts. For much of his time he will be dealing not with large audiences but with individuals looking for guidance on a vast variety of problems – personal, marital, social and professional. As stress within our society increases and neuroses multiply, this side of the minister's work will become more and more important. To handle it helpfully he must be sympathetic and sensitive, human and approachable, firm in his convictions and yet open to the lessons of experience, able to assess people and situations rapidly, unimpeachable in the matter of confidences and able to rebuke without infuriating and to condemn without driving to despair.

Thirdly, the pastor must have preaching gifts. To this end he must have a competent grasp of the Christian message in all its aspects, doctrinal, ethical and experimental. But he must also possess the ability to communicate the message – the quality which Paul defines as 'apt to teach'. This is not the same as being, in today's terms, 'a good communicator'. There is a tension between the art of the rhetorician – 'the enticing words of men's wisdom' – and preaching in the Spirit. Nor does it mean mere fluency. An unceasing verbal torrent can often be aimless, empty and unstructured, serving only to hide from the speaker the poverty of his own thought. The teaching charisma, by contrast, is the ability to express and illustrate the gospel lucidly and cogently.

Paul also insists that the preacher should be able to refute objections to the Christian message (Titus 1:9). Outside the church, believers face an incessant assault on their most basic convictions and although it would be unrealistic (and unbiblical) to expect every pastor to be conversant with the thought of Darwin and Marx, Freud and Heidegger, the pulpit must do all in its power to protect the flock from the chill winds of anti-Christian thought and even to enable the church to carry the battle to the enemy.

Even this brief analysis of the necessary gifts is sufficient to give rise to serious heartsearching on the part of those contemplating the holy ministry. Clearly, no one is adequate to the work. Even John Knox, as we saw, felt himself utterly unprepared and David Brainerd was frequently depressed, 'considering my great unfitness for the work of the ministry, my present deadness and total inability to do anything to the glory of God'. In the last analysis, of course, we gladly recognise that it is not for us to evaluate ourselves and leave it to the church to decide whether it can use us and if so where. But two things we can do. We can stir up – fan into flame – the gifts God has given us; and we can pray to God to increase our gifts, taking courage again from the example of Brainerd, who notes at one point in his diary, 'Was enabled to cry to God with fervency for ministerial qualifications.'

The call of the church
The third step in a vocation to the ministry is the call of the church. This is something we have tended to seriously

underestimate – quite inconsistently. In the case of elders and deacons we have regarded it as decisive and left little to individual initiative. It would be unthinkable for a man suddenly to announce that he was called to be a deacon and expect the church to take the necessary steps to ordination. Admittedly, the problem is complicated today by two factors: the long years of training for the ministry and the expectation that the church will provide for a minister's maintenance. But neither of these can alter the theological fact that ultimately a man is called to the ministry only by the church electing and ordaining him. The individual's preliminary agonising as to his fitness for the work is painful enough. But at the end of it he is still not a minister. He is only a candidate offering himself to the service of the church and professing a willingness to acquiesce in its judgment. If an unfit man finally enters the ministry, the mistake is the church's, not the individual's.

In the practice of the Free Church, the notion of the church's calling must be extended to include not only the final step but all those that lead up to it: preliminary recognition by the Kirk Session, the Presbytery and the General Assembly (through one of its committees); continuous assessment through all the years of training; licensing trials; and, at last, the call from a particular church and ordination to its pastoral oversight.

In these various assessments, the church is bound to look closely at the issues already mentioned: Why does the candidate desire to enter the ministry? And does he possess the gifts necessary for counselling, preaching and leading? But the church must also look at wider issues.

For example, we have no right to ordain a novice. Care must be taken, of course, not to define the concept too narrowly. Paul ordained to the eldership in Galatia men who had been Christians for only a few months (Acts 14:23).

Furthermore, by the time a man comes to be ordained he has invariably been under the scrutiny of the church for several years. It still remains questionable, however, whether it is wise to encourage young men to declare themselves publicly as candidates for the ministry within a few months of their conversion. The same is true of men newly admitted to a particular denomination. There may be much misunderstanding on both sides, and it seems only appropriate to delay ordination until the individual and the church are firmly bonded together.

The church must also look carefully at simple questions of general character, on which the New Testament lays a quite astonishing stress. A man must be blameless as far as outsiders are concerned (1 Tim. 3:7). His life must be free from scandal. He must not be self-willed, obstinate and autocratic. He must not be covetous, irascible or violent. On the contrary, he must be vigilant, disciplined, patient and magnanimous.

Naturally, questions of spiritual character are equally important. It goes without saying that the applicant should be genuinely converted. Yet the question should always be put by the interviewing committee, both because the answer cannot be taken for granted and because if a man cannot tell what God has done for his soul he probably cannot tell anything else. Beyond that, it is clear from Acts 6:3-5 that candidates for the ministry should be 'full of the Holy Spirit and of faith'. Not only *believers* and not only *spiritual* but *full*. They should be eminent in personal piety, fully and habitually under the control of the Spirit. Holy Spirit baptism and Holy Spirit filling are indispensable pre-requisites to biblical ordination.

Again, the church must look at the applicant's reputation as a family man. Specifically: Does he have proper control of his children? Does he bring them up in the knowledge of the Lord? Does he counsel them in the Lord? Or has he by easy-going indifference turned them into sons of Belial, apostate from the church? Or by harsh and inconsistent discipline provoked and estranged them? Does he nourish and cherish his wife and deny himself for her, as Christ did for the church? Does he command her loyalty and respect? And with regard to the extended family: Does he honour his (and his wife's) father and mother? Does he provide for aged and needy relatives (1 Tim. 5:16)? Paul's reasons for asking such questions are devastatingly simple: 'If a man does not know how to run his own house, how can he attend to the church of God?' (1 Tim. 3:5).

Equally important is the question of a man's ability to handle personal relationships. To a large extent, the ministry consists of man-management, and this makes it a potential disaster area for those who are painfully shy, carelessly extrovert or tactless and insensitive. No one who finds it difficult to relate to other human beings can hope to motivate, discipline and inspire so that every talent in a congregation is fully used and individuals of diverse gifts and temperaments are moulded into a harmonious and effective whole.

Finally, the church must be satisfied with the temperament of the candidate. Not that ministers should be expected to have ideal temperaments. One of the assets they bring to their work is sympathy, and that is only possible if they share the susceptibilities of their people. Moreover, some men with fairly serious temperamental problems – for example, the depressive David Brainerd – have been very useful ministers. But the Bible does lay down some very firm guidelines. Those who are short-tempered are ruled out by Paul's insistence that bishops must not be 'soon angry' (Tit. 1:7). Those who are overbearing and arrogant are ruled out by Peter's warning against behaving as if we were 'lords over God's heritage' (1 Pet. 5:3). More broadly, we must surely have serious misgivings about admitting applicants with histories of psychiatric disorders or tendencies that way. There is indeed a place in the ordinary membership of the church for the victims of nervous breakdowns, clinical depression, neurotic anxiety, paranoia and other forms of mental illness. One may even hope that in the Christian fellowship such people will find a comfort and support unavailable elsewhere. But to impose upon them the burdens of ministry is unfair both to them and to the church. The stresses of the pastorate are considerable and may easily induce irretrievable breakdown in those of fragile personality. There is nothing sadder than to see men who might have led perfectly satisfying lives in secular careers broken by pastoral burdens and frustrations they were never equipped to bear. The church, on the other hand, has the right to look to its leaders for strength. If, instead, the pastors themselves are weak, nervous and neurotic, where is the flock to go? A situation can develop all too easily in which the church exhausts itself trying to heal its healers and comfort its comforters.

Our vigilance must be unceasing. Whatever a man's potential to disrupt or deaden the church as an ordinary member, it is increased a hundredfold by ordaining him to the eldership or the ministry. We should be prepared to give every applicant for membership the benefit of the doubt. But as regards the ministry we should be more inclined to act on the opposite principle – to seek not merely an uncontradicted but an accredited profession of a call. 'If he's doubtful he's out.' To spare the flock.

3

PRESBYTERS
AND
PREACHERS

There are two obvious starting-points for any discussion on the question of eldership.

First there are the historic debates within the Reformed tradition itself. These have taken place mainly within American Presbyterianism and have involved some of its greatest theologians – Miller, Thornwell, Dabney and Hodge. These men debated such questions as whether the ruling elder occupies an office distinct from the preaching elder; whether ruling elders may preach; and whether ordination to the eldership should take the same form as ordination to the ministry. To a limited extent these same issues have also been discussed outside the United States, notably by the Irish Presbyterian, Thomas Witherow, and by the Church of Scotland's Panel on Doctrine (which presented a Report on the eldership to the General Assembly in 1964).

The other obvious starting-point is the New Testament vocabulary on the subject. Four words are especially important: *presbuteron*, *episkopos*, *poimēn* and *proestōs*. These terms have a rich background in secular Greek, in the Septuagint, in the synagogue and in the New Testament and their meaning has been thoroughly investigated by New Testament scholars, especially by the Anglicans F. J. A. Hort, J. B. Lightfoot and Edwin Hatch. More recent studies, as reflected, for example, in Kittel's *Theological Dictionary of the New Testament*, have added little to the conclusions of this distinguished trio.

These are the obvious approaches. The trouble with them both is that they lead nowhere, and one is slowly driven to the conclusion that both the theologians and the philologists are asking the wrong questions. The latter approach is by far the more promising. But a church order derived from word-studies alone would be full of confusion and inconsistency. Furthermore, however it might resemble the church of the New Testament in certain details, it would differ from it frighteningly in its overall ethos and organisation. Above all, it would be devoid of any proper ecclesiology of preaching. There is no way we can get from *presbuteros, episkopos, poimēn* or *proestēs* to *the preacher*. Indeed, if this nomenclature exhausts all the church officers available to us today we have no one at all called to the distinctive ministry of the word. It is impossible to reconcile this with the paramount importance of preaching as reflected in, say, the writings of Paul, and this fact itself should alert us to the realisation that our whole approach is wrong. We are not simply coming to the wrong conclusions. We are asking the wrong questions. We must look beyond our inherited church polity and even beyond the lexicographical studies of outstanding New Testament scholars and survey, instead, the basic patterns of organisation and ministry to be found in the apostolic literature.

A sharp distinction

When we do so, the first thing we find is a sharp distinction between those who 'serve tables' and those who give themselves to the ministry of the word. This distinction appears as early as the sixth chapter of Acts. At first, the apostles did everything: the teaching, the administration, the pastoral oversight. But as the church grows, the pressure becomes too great. The apostles protest that it is inappropriate for them to let the distribution of relief encroach on the time needed for the ministry of the word. This led to the appointment of 'the Seven'. They are not specifically called deacons, but their role was certainly diaconal and the narrative will not allow us to belittle it. Those appointed were men of the highest calibre, full of faith and of the Holy Spirit. At least two of the 'deacons', Philip and Stephen, later distinguished themselves as highly effective evangelists. This emphasis on the dignity of the diaconate is maintained throughout the New Testament. Years later, Paul, at the height of his influence and usefulness, sees no threat to his dignity in initiating and organising a collection for the impoverished saints at Jerusalem.

This ministry is surely a permanent one. The church is committed by the Lord to an ongoing ministry to the poor and the organisation of that ministry – as well as the administration of the church's own temporal affairs – will always require men filled with the Spirit. Indeed, the context in Acts strongly suggests that the Seven, as well as the apostles, engaged in a full-time ministry and were maintained by the other members of the church. The need for a full-time diaconate is at least equally urgent today. Indeed, we would do well to ponder the desirability of a trained diaconate as well as a trained teaching ministry; and also the biblical validity of a diaconate of women. The question whether this latter would be an *office* and whether it would require *ordination* would itself be quite alien to the biblical outlook.

The ministry of the Word

But alongside of the ministry of tables there was from the beginning a ministry of the Word, involving both the instruction of those inside the church and the evangelisation of those outside.

This ministry clearly required two things.

First, that a man give himself wholly to it. This was why the apostles did not want to become involved in the problems of administration. They wanted to 'give themselves continually to prayer and to the ministry of the word' (Acts 6:4). It is important to note that the precise business with which the apostles did not wish to be entangled was ecclesiastical. Not even the work of the diaconate should be allowed to distract a preacher of the gospel. How much more does this apply to secular pursuits! It is impossible to engage in an effective preaching ministry if we have to snatch our moments of preparation from the demands of business, trade, politics or the caring professions. Men must give themselves wholly to these matters, devoting themselves single-mindedly to reading, teaching and preaching (1 Tim. 4:13f) – and to prayer (Acts 6:4). They must fan into flame the gift God has given to them (2 Tim. 1:6), making it their foremost determination to be workmen who do not need to be ashamed, correctly handling the word of truth (2 Tim. 2:15). How else can they be prepared to preach the word in season and out of season, correcting, rebuking and encouraging (2 Tim. 4:2)?

There may be times in the history of the modern church, as there were in the days of the apostles, when circumstances force preachers into a part-time ministry. But this is not the biblical pattern. Preaching is no exception to Dr. Johnson's dictum: 'No man ever did anything well to which he did not give the whole bent of his mind.'

The second biblical prerequisite for effective preaching is proper training. This is not highlighted as clearly as the need for total dedication. Yet the emphasis is plain enough. Paul directs Timothy to impart his message to believing and reliable men who will be able to teach others (2 Tim. 2:2). The Twelve were trained by three years' companionship with the Lord. Paul was taken to 'Arabia'. Silas, Mark, Timothy and Titus had Paul himself for their mentor. Preachers are not born. Nor are they the products of mere professional training. They must have the gifts (*charismata*) of knowledge, utterance, wisdom and courage necessary to effective proclamation. But even those with *charismata* need to be trained, learning the message and emulating the methods of their seniors. The precise form which such training will take in particular traditions is a matter of

Christian prudence. But there is great truth in an observation made recently by Dr. Albert Martin: 'Good preaching is contagious.' In view of this, we surely need to re-assess our own practice, whereby divinity students are almost constantly preaching and seldom, if ever, listening.

Mobility of preachers

A second interesting feature of New Testament patterns of ministry is the astonishing mobility of the preachers of the word. At first, the preaching was confined to Jerusalem but after the death of Stephen, persecution scattered the church and the believers went everywhere 'preaching the word' (Acts 8:4). The most notable figure in this movement was Philip, referred to in Acts 21:8 as 'the evangelist'. His ministry was obviously a highly mobile one. One moment he is planting a church in Samaria (Acts 8:5). The next, he is directed by the Lord to go to Gaza. Afterwards, he is found in Azotus and in every city between there and Caesarea. Paul and his companions Barnabas, Silas, Luke and John Mark clearly itinerated equally widely, moving as the Lord directed them into areas where the gospel had not gone before, and deliberately avoiding building on other men's foundations (Rom. 15:20).

Too often the question of an outreach, missionary ministry gets bogged down in debate as to the meaning of *evangelist* and in argument as to whether this 'office' was meant to be permanent. The whole discussion is, surely, irrelevant. There can be no doubt as to the biblical validity of a missionary, church-planting ministry. Nor can there be any doubt as to New Testament precedent for highly mobile, itinerant evangelism. Whatever the nomenclature, an itinerant ministry of the word was clearly integral to New Testament church structures.

The relation of these itinerant preachers to the local church is an interesting one. Whenever the idea of setting up such a ministry is mooted among ourselves, our immediate reaction appears to be to take steps to safeguard the rights of sessions and presbyteries. Before we know where we are the evangelistic function is so shackled and fettered that no self-respecting man could take it on. Nor would he be any use if he did. In the New Testament, by contrast, the controls are minimal. Certainly the local church commissioned Saul and Barnabas (although we cannot be sure that Philip was similarly commissioned). But it is perfectly clear that from that point onwards they were very much on their own. They did not require the permission of 'the sending church' for their movements. With the wisdom given to them by the Holy Spirit they made their own decisions on the spot.

We are too inclined to define leadership in a restrictive sense – exercising control, maintaining order, keeping people in their place. We must learn to see it as something creative and dynamic, inspiring and liberating people to serve, so that no talent and no enthusiasm in the body of Christ goes unused. Only to a very limited extent should one man (or body of men) interfere with another in the spontaneity of his Christian service.

It was not only church-planting missionaries who itinerated, however. In the New Testament many of the church's *teachers* were also highly mobile. This was not, of course, true of them all. The elders appointed by Paul in Galatia were, so far as we can see, local men engaged in a settled ministry. So were those referred to in Acts 20:17ff and in 1 Timothy 5:17. But Timothy and Titus were sent to Ephesus and Crete respectively to teach and to organise the churches already settled there. It is also clear that in the apostolic period prophets and teachers circulated freely, requiring not only hospitality (Rom. 12:13) but also judicious scrutiny (1 John 4:1).

The same mobility should be evident in the church's teachers today. We must be prepared to move anywhere within the worldwide body of Christ according to the leading of the Spirit expressed not in our own private judgments but in the collective wisdom of the church.

Before leaving this point it is worth noting that no hard-and-fast distinction can be drawn between an itinerant and a settled ministry. Itinerants like Paul sometimes settled in particular places for extended periods (Acts 19:10); and sometimes (again like Paul and his associates Timothy and Titus) they exchanged their church-planting roles for church-building ones. The evangelist sometimes became the pastor. Mobility involved flexibility in function as well as in location.

The preachers not presbyters

A still more fascinating aspect of early church structures is that its great preachers were not characteristically elders or presbyters. Some, like Peter and Paul, were apostles. Stephen and Philip belonged to 'the Seven'. Apollos has no official designation. Neither has Titus. Timothy does the work of an evangelist (2 Tim. 4:5). Preachers are described in a quite independent nomenclature as *heralds*, *stewards*, *witnesses* and *ambassadors*, and the attempt to link preaching indissolubly with the presbyterate is quite misguided. There is no hint that all preachers must be presbyters or that all presbyters must be preachers. In fact, the church never depended entirely on the ministry of 'elders'. It always enjoyed a distinctive ministry of preaching engaged in by men who were highly mobile, specially gifted and trained and totally dedicated to proclaiming the gospel. From this point of view, argument about the distinction between *ruling elder* and *teaching elder* leads us down a blind alley.

But this must not lead to a depreciation of the eldership. Presbyters were closely associated with preachers from a very early stage in the history of the church. Paul appointed some in Galatia (Acts 14:23), addressed them at Ephesus (Acts 20:17ff) and directed Titus to establish them in Crete. Their responsibility is broadly defined in the words *episkopos* and *poimēn*. The former means *overseer*, the latter *pastor*. The elders' functions, therefore, were to exercise oversight and to engage in pastoral care.

This involved several different responsibilities, and even when we have put all the New Testament references together, we are probably far from exhausting the range of their activities.

Primarily, they were the leaders or rulers of the congregation. In this respect, they were authority figures, set over the flock (1 Thess. 5:12). They were the men who took the initiative, standing in the van of the church's forward movement, leading by example and taking the flack when their policies were unpopular or simply dangerous.

Again, they were the counsellors, warning, advising and comforting in the light of their own experience and the teaching of Scripture. Today, members of the church take their emotional and behavioural problems to professional psychiatrists – not as a last desperate measure but as a first resort. Does this reflect incompetence on the part of the eldership or a flaunting of New Testament patterns by the membership?

It is also the function of the elders to protect the flock. This is what Paul has especially in mind in Acts 20:29: they must take heed to the flock because grievous wolves threaten it. The peril is both internal and external. Inside, there are false prophets, lying in wait to deceive (Eph. 4:14). Outside, there is the whole range of hostile religion and philosophy. The elders must be able to protect the church in the face of these perils. This is especially true of the internal threat –

Paul's charge to the elders at Ephesus refers particularly to a peril which will arise from 'among your own selves'.

Another element in pastoral care is the need to seek out lost members of the flock. Folk fall by the wayside for all kinds of reasons – persecution, the cares of this world, personal backsliding, apathy, misunderstanding. Such people constitute only a tiny fraction of the church as a whole but they need a quite disproportionate amount of attention. Like the Good Shepherd Himself, the Christian elder/pastor will leave the ninety-and-nine and go to look for the one lost sheep. In theory, it may seem fair enough to promise every single member of the flock an equal degree of care. In practice this would be absurd. The lame, the weak, the wounded and the stray always clamour for attention, and it becomes as impossible to 'run' a church to a timetable as it would be to run a medical practice.

Paul also stipulates that elders are to be 'given to hospitality' (1 Tim. 3:2). In its simplest form this means that all Christians are welcome in the elders' homes. If need be, the local church can even hold its meetings there, as it did in Chloe's house (1 Cor. 1:11). But the real point of Paul's principle is probably more specialised. As we have seen, the church was both nourished and propagated through the ministry of a highly mobile band of preachers, and in their journeyings these men would naturally require accommodation. Paul expects that the responsibility for providing it would gladly be assumed by the elders. It would be a mistake, however, to think that it devolved on them alone. The Writer to the Hebrews exhorts his readers to entertain strangers, and even holds out the inducement that by making a general rule of this they may some day entertain angels unawares (Heb. 13:2).

It is more difficult to evaluate the function indicated in James 5:14: 'Is any sick among you? Let him call for the elders of the church; and let them pray over him, anointing him with oil in the name of the Lord.' What exactly is meant by the reference to oil is very difficult to say. But the general sense of the passage is clear: It is the responsibility of elders to minister to the sick and the precise form of their ministry is to pray for them. It is not the oil that heals but believing prayer (verse 15). The stipulation that the sick person should *send* for the elders should not be abused. To claim the excuse, 'We were not sent for!' would be contrary to the whole spirit of the gospel.

Elders and teaching

To what extent was teaching an inherent function of the eldership? Paul makes it plain in 1 Timothy 5:17 that not all elders laboured in the word and in teaching. The background to this is probably the same sentiment as we saw in Acts 6:2: an effective ministry of the word can only be engaged in by a man who lays aside every other responsibility and devotes himself to the word of God and prayer. This was clearly not expected of all elders.

On the other hand, they were all expected to be 'apt to teach' (*didaktikos*): and in Ephesians 4:11 pastoral care and teaching are closely linked. We should not read too much into this, however. Neither the gift of teaching nor the responsibility of teaching was all that distinctive. Deacons, too, must hold the mystery of the faith with a pure conscience (1 Tim. 3:9). Older women are to *teach* younger women (Titus 2:4) and the whole congregation are to *teach* one another in psalms, hymns and spiritual songs (Col. 3:16). The responsibility of all mature Christians towards the immature is clearly illustrated in the way that Priscilla and Aquila looked after Apollos, teaching him the way of the Lord more perfectly (Acts 18:26). Every Christian must confess his faith (Rom. 10:9; Heb. 4:14) and be able to give to all those who ask a reason for his hope (1 Pet. 3:15).

Indeed, the very significance of Pentecost is that, at last, all the people are prophets (Acts 2:17), witnessing to Christ (Acts 1:8) and proclaiming the virtues of the One who called them out of darkness into His own marvellous light (1 Pet. 2:9).

All this suggests that *aptness to teach* was a widespread gift in the apostolic church. It was certainly not enough in itself to constitute a man an elder. It had no more weight in this connection than any of the other qualities referred to by Paul (1 Tim. 3:1ff). To put it bluntly: A man has no more right to be an elder simply because he can teach than he has because he is the husband of one wife. The indispensable teaching gift that Paul was looking for probably amounted to no more than an ability to bear a clear personal witness to Christ, to answer objectors and to give adequate pastoral counsel. What was desirable in all Christians was indispensable in an elder.

There is no significance in the fact that elders are required to be apt to *teach* rather than apt to *preach*. The New Testament does not regard preaching and teaching as technically distinct. The Sermon on the Mount, for example, is regarded as teaching: 'Jesus opened his mouth and *taught* them' (Matt. 5:2). Similarly, when the Lord commissions the disciples to evangelise the nations, He directs them to *teach* all the things He Himself has commanded (Matt. 28:20). Whether in a pastoral or in an evangelistic setting, therefore, preaching must be didactic. For the pulpit to neglect doctrine is calamitous.

General points

Two points of more general interest deserve brief notice.

First, elders were supported by their local congregations. This was plainly so in the case of those who were not only elders but also preachers. It also applied, however, to at least some of those who were simply elders. According to most scholars, when Paul says in 1 Timothy 5:17 that the elders who rule well should receive double *honour* he is probably referring to double *remuneration*. Certainly, the primary meaning of the Greek word used (*timē*) is *price* or *value* and the meaning *honorarium* is well established. The interesting thing in 1 Timothy 5:17, however, is that Paul is speaking not of preachers but of those who 'rule well'. It is they who are to be counted worthy of double remuneration. We have already seen that a good biblical case can be made out for a full-time, paid diaconate. An equally good case can be made for maintaining some elders in a full-time ministry.

Secondly, the authority of elders was not confined to their own congregations. For example, the elders who gathered at the Council of Jerusalem (Acts 15:6ff) were clearly making decisions which bound the whole church. But the question is not one merely of the use of the word *elder*. The truth as to the nature of Christian oversight can no more be gathered from the word *presbyter* than can the truth as to preaching. We must look at the whole authority structure of the New Testament church. From the very beginning the church had a unified, collegiate leadership extending to all its congregations. That leadership was directly involved and consulted at every critical point in the development of the emerging people of God: the reception of the Samaritan church (Acts 8:14), Peter's mission to Cornelius (Acts 11:1ff) and Paul's ministry to the Gentiles (Gal. 2:9). The idea of totally isolated, fully autonomous churches is wholly alien to the New Testament. The church is the body of Christ, one in mission and one in its visible expression. Each member is united not only to the Head but to each other member.

At the moment, the Reformed churches in Great Britain present a very different picture. They are so fragmented as to suggest that Christ has a thousand-and-one bodies. This is frequently true even in very narrow local contexts – in fact, we are often more prepared to fraternise with brethren thousands of miles across the sea than with those on our own doorsteps. The public image this gives us is disastrous and the effect on our efficiency is even worse. Hire-and-fire churches, where the pastor has less security than a pub pianist, proliferate. Local oligarchies arise, jealous only for their own position. There is a total lack of cohesion in home and foreign missions, in the training and settlement of ministers and in the administration of discipline. The fugitives from one church are too often the proudly displayed trophies of another.

Surely the time has come for all the Reformed churches to come together, to the very limits of their respective polities. Deliberative assemblies are not enough – indeed, if we want to be strictly biblical, we have no New Testament warrant whatever for mere talking-shops. We need an organic unity, committed to the Reformed faith and clearly recognising that we can no longer divorce the doctrine of the church from effective evangelism and pastoral care. An anarchic church, pulling in a thousand different directions, plagued by factions and preyed upon by empire-builders is both an inept and an unworthy instrument for Christ's mission to the world.

A Shibboleth[1]

Eldership has become a shibboleth in many churches which have recently discovered the Reformed faith. Indeed, it has become a badge of orthodoxy and some brethren have succumbed to the temptation to push the issue beyond what their churches will bear. This is a tragic mistake. If we have elders under another name (deacons!), let us be content. It

1 Judges 12:6 - A word or phrase which signify's ones attachment to a particular grouping.

is the ministry itself that matters, not its designation. Furthermore, if the church is reluctant, ministers should not push the issue. We cannot reform the church by breaking it. No man with the heart of a shepherd will blow his flock to smithereens.

Above all, if independent churches are to have elders, it is vital that their position be clearly defined, especially in relation to the pastor. It should be clearly understood from the outset that labouring in the word and doctrine is not an essential part of the elder's ministry, that those engaged in a preaching ministry should be specifically trained for it and that they should give themselves wholly to it. Conversely, if a man is convinced that he has a call to be a preacher, he should indicate his willingness to renounce his secular employment and to submit to whatever training the church prescribes. If these things are clearly understood from the outset, the most fruitful cause of friction and heartbreak will be removed.

We return, then, to our basic perspective. The New Testament applies a wide variety of designations to the various functionaries of the church. Some are technical, but most are not, and few, if any, are used with elaborate precision and accuracy. There are certainly not as many ministries as designations and it is quite impossible to deduce any clear idea of church-structures from the terminology alone. The truth can only be found by trying to identify the various ministries enjoyed by the apostolic church. These were threefold: A ministry of tables, a ministry of oversight and a ministry of preaching. All of these transcended local churches; representatives of all of them might be fully maintained; and the preachers were expected to be highly mobile.

4

THE
PRIMACY
OF
PREACHING

As long ago as 1848 Hugh Miller lamented that it had become the fashion in the Free Church to speak of preaching as 'not the paramount but merely one of the subsidiary duties of the clergyman'.

The trend was evident in three different connections.

First, it governed attitudes to incumbent ministers. '"He is not a man of much pulpit preparation", it has become common to remark of some minister, at least liked if not admired, but he is diligent in visiting and in looking after his schools; and preaching is in reality but a small part of a minister's duty." '

Secondly, it governed the attitude of vacant congregations. 'The flock looking out for a pastor are apt enough to say, "Our last minister was an accomplished pulpit man, but what we at present want is a man sedulous in visiting; for preaching is in reality but a small part to a minister's duty." '

Thirdly, it governed the attitude to preaching of ministers themselves: 'Ministers, especially ministers of but a few twelve months' standing, have themselves in some cases caught up with the remark as if it embodied a self-evident truth; and while they dare tell, not without self-complacency, that their discourses cost them but little trouble, they add further, as if by way of apology, that they are, however, much occupied otherwise and that preaching is in reality but a small part of a minister's duty. We have sometimes felt inclined to assure these latter personages in reply that they might a little improve the matter just by making preaching no part of their duty at all.'

Preaching does, of course, have a paramount place both in Scripture and in the Standards of the Free Church. According to the Shorter Catechism, for example, it is especially the preaching of the word that the Spirit uses to convert sinners and to build them up in the faith (Answer 89). The commission given to the apostles was to go and teach the nations (Matt. 28:19). The Holy Spirit was given at Pentecost precisely to enable the church to proclaim the wonderful works of God (Acts 2:11). And Paul makes it abundantly clear that he regards preaching as his supreme task. He rejoices that God sent him not to baptise but to preach the gospel (1 Cor. 1:17); he affirms that it is through the foolishness of preaching that God saves (1 Cor. 1:21); and he indicates that the hallmark of a faithful pastor is that he labours in the word and in teaching (1 Tim. 5:17).

Practical implications

Miller's remarks are as valid today as they were when he wrote them. Both the pulpit and the pew should lay them to heart and give urgent heed to their practical implications.

For example, the primacy of preaching must govern our approach to the selection of candidates for the ministry. Not that preaching ability is the only consideration. Health, motives, education, personal relationships, piety and practical spiritual experience are obviously of enormous importance. But all is useless if the applicant cannot preach, because that is to be the major part of his life's work. Yet in practice this is a question to which we pay little attention. Some are accepted as candidates for the ministry although they have never preached – this was certainly true in my own case. It might have been notorious enough that I could blether, but no one had any right to believe that I could preach. It is true, of course, that by the time a student comes to be licensed considerable trial has been made of his preaching gifts. But surely this concern should be paramount from the beginning and only in very rare instances should presbyteries accept candidates who have no preaching experience at all.

It is even more important that our conviction as to the primacy of preaching should govern the curriculum we lay down for the training of ministers. Modern theological institutions have little interest in preparing men to be heralds of salvation. Their products are usually amalgams of psychiatrists, entertainers and social workers. Even thoroughly Reformed seminaries are placing too much emphasis on irrelevant academic study and modern counselling techniques, sometimes with incongruous results, as in the case of the preacher who solemnly announced to his Sunday evening congregation, 'Our subject tonight is, *The Problem of the Authorship of Second Peter.*' Preachers are primarily expositors and the most important part of their training is that which deals with biblical interpretation.

The dignity and authority of preaching

Another consequence of the primacy of preaching is that the preacher must assert the independent dignity and authority of his own role within the life of the church. For too long the pew has dictated to the pulpit. In its extreme form this has given rise to the movement for demythologising the gospel. Bultmann and his co-adjutors have asked modern man what he finds credible; and in response to his answer they have eliminated from the message everything that savours of the supernatural. The result is an emasculated religion, credible enough, but so banal and mundane as to be worthless. We have, mercifully, been spared these calamities. But there have been others. For example, there has been the demand for brevity. Our people have declared their impatience with long sermons and have laid down limits beyond which they are not prepared to listen. Some congregations have said 30 minutes, some 20 and some even less. There is, of course, no virtue in length for its own sake, and we offer no defence of the tediousness, prolixity and long-windedness from which preaching has often suffered. It seems curious, however, that Christians are prepared to sit for hours in front of television screens imbibing the most supine drivel, yet find three-quarters of an hour of biblical exposition unendurable. Have such people ever tasted the goodness of the word of God? Preachers are ambassadors, plenipotentiaries invested with the authority of Christ. They have a message to deliver, whether men will hear or whether they will forbear, and a right to claim as much of their people's time as they need to deliver that message and drive home its lessons.

The pew has also demanded simplicity and again the prophets have yielded too readily. Certainly, lucidity is important. The preacher must choose his vocabulary with care, he must arrange his message logically and he must be at pains to show that the various points which he makes follow naturally from the words of his text. But simplicity is something else. It is a straitjacket into which the gospel simply will not fit. It means the banishment of doctrine from the pulpit, a non-theological evangelism and a generation of Christians who have no idea what they believe. To many of our people, such doctrines as the trinity, the incarnation and the atonement are closed books. The need is not for the exposition of simple themes, laced with anecdotes and seasoned with histrionics, but for the lucid exposition of the riches of revelation. Each Lord's Day, congregations should be led to the point where they cry, 'Oh! the depth!' And if they are not – if we have robbed the gospel of the great elements of mystery and wonder and depth and paradox – then we have failed in our mission and cheated our people. Men may laugh. They may gnash their teeth. But the only message we have a right to preach is one so astonishing that angels desire to look into it and so profound that they have to stoop to do so.

The preacher must equally assert his independence and authority in rebuking sin. The Free Church is only too well known as a denouncing church and, no doubt, the reputation is deserved. The trouble is that the denunciations are not always well-directed. Too often they are aimed at those who are not within hearing and whom it therefore costs us nothing to offend. Our people are perfectly willing to lap up condemnations of Catholics, Modernists, politicians, trade-unionists and the permissive society, from all of which they feel comfortably distanced. What they do not welcome is exposure of their own particular sins: traditionalism, worldliness, niggardliness, lukewarmness, complacency and pettiness. The real test of a preacher is not the eloquence with which he denounces the Pope and the Prince of Wales (neither of whom is likely to be in his congregation) but the faithfulness with which he rebukes the ungraciousness of his own elders, members and adherents. We magnify our office by telling *our own people* what they do not want to hear.

Keeping other commitments to a minimum

It also follows from the primacy of preaching that ministers must keep their commitments in other spheres to a minimum. 'No one ever did anything well,' said Dr. Johnson, 'to which he did not give the whole bent of his mind.'

It is, of course, easy to claim that we have so much else to attend to that there is no time for proper pulpit preparation. For example, there is pastoral visitation, a part of our ministry which it would be foolish to belittle. In a church-extension context this is the only way to establish the vital initial contact. In normal pastoral work it is an indispensable ministry to the sick, the lapsed and those who need individual counselling. On the other hand, our consciences surely bear witness that not all the time spent out of the study is given to visiting; nor is all our visiting rigorously pastoral. A man is no more a good pastor because he visits frequently than he is a good preacher because he preaches often. Furthermore, few of us can claim that we spend our forenoons in pastoral visitation. Indeed, there is no reason why every minister in the Church should not spend the hours from nine to one in his study. Nor should we overlook the fact that the pastoral responsibility does not belong to the minister alone. It is shared by all the other elders who are, by definition, co-pastors, and if men are not prepared to visit the sick and the lapsed and to counsel the weak they should not be elders in the first place.

The problem has another side. Suppose a minister gives his whole attention to visiting, what is the most he can expect? That the people will come to church. But then suppose that in gratitude for his visit – *to support 'the poor body'* – they do come to hear him preach, what will they hear, if he has given himself no time for adequate preparation and preaches a loose, rambling sermonette totally lacking in cohesion or interest, a discourse in which there is nothing new for the mind, nothing majestic for the emotions and nothing stimulating for the will? 'No apology whatever ought to be sustained for imperfect pulpit preparation,' wrote Hugh Miller: 'People neither ought nor will misspend their Sabbaths in dozing under sermons to which no effort of attention, however honestly made, enables them to listen.' It is pointless to visit with a view to encouraging people to come to church if, when they do come, they are not presented with a message which compels their attention and demands decision.

The situation is aggravated in some areas of the Church by the ministrations which people have come to expect from ministers at times of bereavement. Not so long ago it was enough that the minister conduct the funeral service (having already, of course, met with the family privately as soon as possible after he heard of their sorrow). It was left to the district elders to conduct family worship in the homes on the preceding evenings. Now it is expected that the minister attend 'the wake' (what a pagan term!) each evening; if he does not he has to face the embarrassment of the likely presence of ministers from other congregations only too willing to take his place and expose him to the charge of heartless negligence. The result, in our larger congregations, is that ministers are employed in this way almost every evening of the week. How can we claim to have no time for pulpit preparation while yet feeling perfectly free to waste large tracts of time intruding into other congregations? And what are our elders worth if we cannot leave these meetings in their hands? In fact, we are in grave danger of generating a new brand of superstition in connection with our death-rites. We have moved back unthinkingly into the situation deprecated by Chalmers during his Glasgow ministry, when he found that no respectable citizen was deemed decently buried unless at least seven or eight ministers attended his funeral. In one intriguing recent instance when a minister was unable to conduct a funeral personally and entrusted it to a student, the relatives were most put out and even ventured to express doubts as to whether the deceased were *legally* buried. What next?

Another danger is that we can become enmeshed in the webs of ecclesiastical bureaucracy. Committees appear to be *doing* things. One can see apparently tangible results and enjoy the illusion of power. Of course we need administration and there is no necessary conflict between the existence of committees and the great principles of presbyterian church government. Certainly church-power must remain with the courts which the New Testament sanctions. But in our system it is these very courts which in their wisdom appoint committees to expedite their business. We can, however, have an excess of administration and some of our present committees are frankly useless). Some men are on too many committees; and some – notably ministerial clerks – are too deeply involved in particular committees. No minister of the gospel has the right to allow anything to make serious inroads into the time available to him for pulpit preparation. Nor have we any right to leave the word of God and serve tables. The work of our committees is largely diaconal and we should leave as much of it as possible to laymen. Indeed the Church should have a limited full-time diaconate, preferably with some theological training, but majoring in administration. In effect this is what our office staff are. The trouble is that we do not project it as a distinctive Christian vocation, especially for the women of the Church, many of whom are perfectly capable of clerking our Committees and thus releasing ministers for the specific work to which God has called them.

What is true of ministerial involvement in church bureaucracy applies with even greater force to politics. Local government is no place for a minister. It leads to an endless series of embarrassments, compromises and temptations. It seems to say that we believe in the primacy of the seen and temporal over the unseen and eternal. It makes totally inadmissible demands on a preacher's time. It is a flagrant defiance of the apostolic principle that we should not entangle ourselves in the affairs of this life.

Centrality in all worship

One final implication of the primacy of preaching deserves mention: we must not displace it from its central position in every gathering of the worshipping church. In Catholic traditions the sacraments have frequently usurped the place of the sermon. In charismatic churches the exercise of spiritual gifts has done the same. Within modernism, churches emptied by insipid platitudes make a desperate attempt to win back congregations by providing brighter services: brighter not by brighter preaching but by replacing preaching with dialogue, drama, film-shows and the like. The Free Church seems to be free from these distortions. This is not to say, however, that in the case of the Free Church the Devil has been inactive. He has come in as an angel of light and brought about a situation whereby in many areas prayer-meetings have replaced the preaching of the word on Lord's Day evenings. Many motives have operated, of course: the anti-clericalism of the Highlands, anxious to show that worship can proceed perfectly well without a minister; the ambition of elders to take a more prominent (which is not the same as a more useful) place in the services of the Church; local jealousy, determined to hang on to village meeting-houses long after modern transport has made them obsolete; and the plausible pseudo-spirituality which argues that prayer-meetings are more beneficial than preaching services. Whatever the motives, the results have been calamitous.

Every Lord's Day evening, hundreds, if not thousands, of Free Church people on Skye and Lewis meet with no minister to preside over them and, what is worse, no sermon to listen to; while, a few miles away, preachers proclaim the gospel to empty pews. People – Christian people – who regularly travel 20 or 30 miles to work will not travel a mile to listen to a sermon. It is not surprising that adherents brought up on such spiritual fare are spiritually and theologically illiterate. They have never heard expository preaching or the intelligent assertion, maintenance and defence of the gospel. They know little at all of the distinctive principles of their own Church. It is hardly surprising either, that many young people, unprepared to suffer the agony (for them) of standing through five long prayers have long since ceased to attend; or that when they move to the mainland their loyalty to the Church is far too shallow and far too uncomprehending to withstand the shock of exposure to the prevailing godlessness.

No wonder we have lost the Highlands! And unless urgent steps are taken we shall lose the Islands too. In the past, fear of local opposition has stifled every attempt to gather our people into the main preaching centres on Lord's Day evenings. It is no easy thing to face up to elders who place personal and local considerations before the spiritual well-being of their people. But the choice is between that and extinction.

'I have no patience,' wrote the late Rev. Kenneth MacRae, 'with that spirit which sees any change in connection with services or meetings as a sin. This unreasoning, unreasonable spirit which refuses religion the right to adapt itself to the changed circumstances in which it may find itself has done infinite harm in the Highlands. It seems to think that it is better to die in a rut than to try to get out of it. It is strange too, how good people can be the main hindrance to every fresh effort to advance the Lord's cause.'

5

PREACHING
FROM THE
OLD TESTAMENT

If a young preacher wants to preach from the New Testament he can easily find models. He has only to read the published expositions of Dr. Lloyd-Jones and John Stott to see master craftsmen at work in a contemporary idiom. The situation with regard to the Old Testament is quite different. It is often difficult to find even competent commentaries on the Old Testament. From any given part of the New Testament, one can easily find three of four masterpieces of insight and scholarship. By contrast, there are many books of the Old Testament for which not one single good commentary exists.

Underlying this there is something deeper. The hermeneutical barriers which separate us from the world of the Old Testament are enormous. Everything is on a grander scale than the difficulties of New Testament exposition. The time is more remote. The language is more alien. The culture is more unfamiliar.

Absolute authority

Can we find any general principles to guide us?

First of all, we can plant our feet firmly on the rock of the absolute authority of the Old Testament. It was precisely these holy scriptures that Paul described as 'inspired'. Curiously, he does not say that the writers were inspired. He says that the books were inspired. They were breathed out by God. Nor is this true merely of some portions of the Old Testament. It was *all* inspired. Some parts may be less interesting, less majestic and even less useful than others. But every single part is inspired. What any Old Testament scripture says, God says.

This means at once that the entire Old Testament must be handled with reverence. It is all 'holy'. It also means that the preacher has to interpret it harmonistically. He cannot set one part against another. Nor can he contrast any part of it with the truth. As a word from God, it must hang together coherently and harmonise with all that we know from other sources.

For the same reason the preacher knows that the whole Old Testament is profitable. Its value is co-extensive with its inspiration. This applies even to those parts of it which have been superseded, such as the civil law of Israel and the cultic arrangements associated with Tabernacle and Temple. The detailed instructions laid down in these connections are no longer binding on the church. Yet they still serve to illustrate, symbolise and typify important truths, and the statutes of the theocracy can serve as paradigms to indicate how the principles of the Ten Commandments should be applied in specific political situations.

The unity of biblical religion

The second important general principle is the unity of biblical religion. The whole of Scripture is a revelation of the one God, disclosing one single scheme of redemption and one covenant of grace. However important the transition from the Old Testament to the New, the parties, the promises and the stipulations of the covenant remain the same. Similarly, the church of God is one under both dispensations. The New Testament church is not a new church – instead, the Gentiles are grafted into the existing people of God, the stock of Abraham. We have Abraham's faith. We are Abraham's seed. It is because of this that the New Testament church can be described in terms lifted straight out of the Old Testament: we are a chosen generation, a royal priesthood, a holy nation, a peculiar people (1 Pet. 2:9).

One immediate result of this is that we can take an *exemplarist* approach to preaching the Old Testament. These saints were under the same ethic and subject to the same experiences as ourselves. The criticisms urged against them by God are still relevant today. Their moods are our moods, their perplexities our perplexities, their aspirations our aspirations. God's call to Abraham we can parallel from our own experience. His anguish as God tries his faith we can follow in our own souls. We can understand Moses as he resists God's call and protests, 'I am not eloquent.' We have often sat with Elijah under his juniper tree. We admire the compassion of Job as he cries, 'The Lord gave and the Lord hath taken away. Blessed be the name of the Lord.' But we can also follow him, in all the utterances of his impatience and frustration as he struggles, often unsuccessfully, to accept the will of God. What terrible utterances they are! God destroys the perfect as well as the wicked! He laughs at the trial of the innocent! 'If I wash myself with snow water, and make my hands never so clean, yet shalt thou plunge me in the ditch, and mine own clothes shall abhor me' (Job 9:30-31).

Of course, our calling is to be content, cheerful and thankful. But how marvellously encouraging it is to know, on those days when we cannot understand and cannot shrug off the pain and cannot hold back our own bitterness, that our complaints do not put us outwith the people of God. And how instructive it is, too, to look at the failings of these great Old Testament men of God. What a rebuke to our complacency to realise what happened to Moses and David and Solomon and Jonah. Yet, in a strange (and always dangerous) way, how comforting! Ungodly men and sometimes appalling failures, and yet God did not cast them off.

The differences in culture, temperament and theological insight which separate us from these men are enormous. Yet the things that unite us are far greater than those which divide us, and the record of their struggles is one of the most precious possessions of the New Testament church.

Progressive revelation

Yet there is a third principle – the progressiveness of revelation – which pulls us in the exactly opposite direction by reminding us of the distinctions between the two administrations of the covenant. God did not reveal Himself all at once. Instead, He gave us a great series of cumulative acts of self-disclosure, speaking 'at sundry times and in divers manners'. This never means that the later revelation contradicts the earlier, but it does mean that some doctrines which are very clear and prominent in the New Testament receive very little emphasis in the Old. For example, the Law and the Prophets contain virtually nothing on the resurrection of the body, the state of the soul between death and judgement or the doctrine of hell. Nor does the earlier revelation contain any overall doctrine of the Person of Christ. All the ingredients for a doctrine are there: the deity of Messiah, the humanity of Messiah, His suffering, His humiliation and His victory. But no one in the Old Testament ever put these strands together to say, 'God will become flesh.' Nor did anybody ever synthesise the concepts of the Suffering Servant and the Son of Man, as our Lord Himself did when He said, 'the Son of Man came to give his life a ransom for many.'

In view of these considerations, the preacher must avoid ascribing to the saints of the Old Testament more light than they actually possessed. Augustine's famous illustration should remain with us. He compared the Old Testament to a room fully furnished but unlit. The occupants cannot see the contents because of the darkness. These become visible only in the light of the New Testament. That light puts nothing there which was not there before. But it does enable us to see adumbrations of the sacrifice of Christ, intimations of a blessed immortality and even hints of the doctrine of the trinity. Those who had only the light of the Old Testament could not see these things and it is anachronistic to read them back into their experiences. David in Psalm 51 had a very clear grasp of the mercy of God, but there is no indication that he saw that that mercy would operate through the blood of One who was God's own Son.

A further important result of the progressiveness of revelation is that we must emphasise much more than we do the superiority of the position of New Testament saints. We seem to have lost sight almost completely of the point made by Paul in Galatians 3:23–4:7. Before Christ came, he says, believers were like children, under the care of a Guardian (the Law) and in many respects no better-off than slaves. Not only did they lack much of the insight of New Testament believers, they lacked much of their comfort. It was much more difficult then to cry, 'Abba! Father,' or to come with boldness to the throne of grace. It was difficult – much more difficult – to face death with confidence. Instead of Paul's, 'I have a desire to depart and to be with Christ, which is far better,' we have David's, 'For in death there is no remembrance of thee; in Sheol, who can give thee praise?' (Ps. 6:5).

Above all, the Old Testament was a time of bondage. The Custodian was everywhere, interfering with what one ate, what one wore, what one sowed, how one ploughed, how one built a house. Life was circumscribed with endless restrictions. Indeed, it was virtually impossible to move without stumbling against an ordinance. From all this, Christ liberated His church, a point which our own Confession brings out admirably: 'Under the New Testament, the liberty of Christians is further enlarged in their freedom from the yoke of the ceremonial law, to which the Jewish church was subjected, and in greater boldness of access to the throne of grace, and in fuller communications of the free Spirit of God, than believers under the law did ordinarily partake of.'

This great fact must come out – and come out prominently – in our preaching. We are no longer slaves, but sons: 'Stand fast, therefore, in the freedom with which Christ has made us free' (Gal. 5:1). Even as we thank God for the inspired word of the Old Testament we are called upon to praise Him for the fact that we are not Old Testament believers. There are indeed parts of the Old Testament from which the very conclusion to be drawn by the preacher must be, 'Thank God that things are different now.'

The nature of prophecy

It is even more important for the preacher to have a firm grasp of the true nature of prophecy. We have tended to see the prophets too narrowly as foretellers and our expositions focus almost exclusively on their predictions. They were, of course, foretellers, and we have no wish to minimise this. But they were much more. They were forth-tellers, men who had been summoned into God's presence, told His secret (or 'mystery') and commissioned to be His spokesmen. Sometimes their message was a prediction, but more often it was not. The fact that Moses was the greatest of the prophets should alert us to this. His messages were hardly ever predictive. He came forth from the Presence with great doctrines such as the unity of God (Deut. 6:4); and with a massive statement of the Law of God, involving great moral principles, complex cultic ordinances and detailed civil statutes. The same is true of the other prophets. More often than not, they were bearers of weighty doctrinal and ethical messages. Indeed even when they are predictive, their predictions can be traps for the unwary preacher. Much of what they say about the last days does not refer to the end-time at all, but to the New Testament era, marked as the age of fulfilment by the incarnation of the Son and the coming of the Spirit.

But maybe the most important fact for the expositor of the prophets is that the great bulk of Old Testament prophecy consists of God's critical evaluation of the church. There are vast tracts which contain only indictment and arraignment of the people of God and if we go to them looking for predictions, Christology and clever allegories we shall go hopelessly wrong. Even in such a prophet as Hosea, with his matchless portrayal of the love and mercy and faithfulness of God, the judgmental element is uppermost: 'Your love is like the morning mist, like the early dew that disappears. Therefore I cut you in pieces with my prophets, I killed you with the words of my mouth; my judgments flashed like lightning upon you' (Hos. 6:4, 5). This was the nature of prophecy from the first, a fact upon which the perceptive Ahab laid his finger when he called Elijah 'the troubler of Israel'. Was the same not true of our Lord Himself, with His great denunciations of the Pharisees? Indeed, even after His resurrection was it not the same word – the word of judgment – which he sent to the Seven Churches by His servant John? 'I have something against you!'

When we are thinking of doing a series of sermons on one of the prophets, this is something we must ponder carefully. If we are going to be faithful to our text, our sermons are going to be critical and judgmental; and if we are going to expound consecutively, this is the diet our people are going to have for weeks on end. The question is: Do they need it? When John Knox preached on Daniel at the Reformation, the church needed it. The Abomination of Desolation was only too obviously active. Similarly, in many mainline churches still, there is unfaithfulness to God on a massive scale. Similarly also, in the society of our own day there is acquisitiveness, disloyalty, exploitation and oppression. In all such situations, the message of the prophets is singularly appropriate, provided a man has the courage to preach it. But before we decide to give our own congregations the same fare, we must be sure that they, too, need, in Hosea's words, to be 'cut and killed'. Are they apostate idolaters, guilty of deceit and violence, resting on formal religious observances while at the same time violating all the commandments of God?

We stand, as preachers, between the world and the word. We must know the world, especially our own particular segment of it. Otherwise we shall find ourselves accusing pious old ladies of 'selling their souls to many lovers'.

A primary source

Two points in conclusion.

First, the Old Testament is our primary source for the knowledge of many doctrines. On such topics as the attributes of God, creation and the nature of man, it is far fuller than the New Testament. Indeed, one of the grave dangers in neglecting the Old Testament is that we shall produce a generation of Christians gravely deficient in their knowledge of all these fundamental matters. Nor is the problem confined to doctrine. The great bulk of biblical teaching on the subjective and experiential side of Christianity is also to be found in the Old Testament. It is there – particularly in Psalms, Job and Jeremiah – that we see reflected the inner moods and struggles of the people of God. To ignore this vein of revelation will lead inevitably either to a superficial religion or to blank incomprehension when we find God trying our faith.

The earlier revelation also contains most of the biblical teaching on the world and our attitude to it. Compared with the New Testament, the Old is earthy, and that earthiness is an indispensable element in revelation. It tells us to subdue and colonise the earth; to be fruitful and multiply; to till the soil and keep our gardens; to name and classify the animals. It shows us men drinking wine, playing their harps and singing songs. It shows us men like Daniel, mastering pagan learning, rising to the top in the world's greatest bureaucracy and eventually becoming the leading politician of a decadent empire – all without defiling himself. It shows us the dignity of the shepherd and the artisan, the legitimacy of the military and the God-givenness of architectural and artistic skill. None of that is rescinded in the New Testament. Indeed, much of it is reiterated. But it was because the Reformed church was so deeply rooted in the Old Testament that Abraham Kuyper could say of it, 'The avoidance of the world has never been the Calvinistic mark but the shibboleth of the Anabaptist.'

Finally, the danger of a false Christocentrism. It is very well to say that Christ is everywhere in the Old Testament and that what we must take out of every text is the contribution it makes to God's revelation of Him. But sometimes those who approach the Old Testament like this are scornful of exemplarist (or as they would call it, *moralising*) preaching. They would argue that you must not use narrative texts to teach merely ethical lessons. Such stories as David and Goliath, they say, are not there to moralise, but to extend the horizons of salvation history.

The trouble with this is that it does not square with the way the New Testament uses the Old. What are we to make, for example, of the Lord's words to His disciples, 'Remember Lot's wife!'? Furthermore, the procedure misconceives Christ's relation to the Old Testament. It is safer to say that He is everywhere *behind* it than to say that He is everywhere *in* it. Every preacher must come to his people with 'the mind of Christ'. But when Paul made that claim for himself, he was not preaching Christology. He was giving elementary directions with regard to the place of women in the church. Yet he was still 'preaching Christ' because he was expressing *His* mind.

The basic principle here must surely be: Every word in the Old Testament is *from* Christ, but not every word is *about* Christ. If so, then we are as surely preaching Christ when

we draw inferences from the politics of Solomon as we are
when faithfully expounding the 53rd chapter of Isaiah.

6

CAN THE CHURCH GROW?

Christ and His apostles clearly expected the church to grow. The mustard seed would become a great tree (Matt. 13:32). The body would grow to the size of a mature man (Eph. 4:13). By contrast, many of us seem to think that small is beautiful: or at least, that growth is none of our business. It will come about by revival, without effort, outreach or invitation on our part.

It would be foolish, not to say heretical, to ignore the grain (and more) of truth in this point of view. Without divine blessing and renewal, growth is impossible. Furthermore, there is always a danger that we try to force growth: or to fake it. It is not difficult to secure professions of conversion, packed churches and an enlarged Communion Roll. A certain amount of scepticism towards what is commonly called *church growth* is fully justified.

But the pre-occupation with revival which prevails in some quarters is at least equally dangerous. Presumably a revived church is a living one. If revival is something occasional and exceptional, does that mean that a living church is also something occasional and exceptional? That can hardly be the case. A church through which the Spirit of God blows as 'a rushing, mighty wind', stimulating men and women to proclaim the mighty works of God (Acts 2:2), is a *normal* church. By the same token, a church which plods along, staid, jaded, stagnant, unadventurous and unexciting, is a church in a highly unusual condition, betraying all the signs of being spiritually moribund. Growth and effectiveness are the marks of an ordinary, living Christian congregation. How could it be otherwise if we have a message which is God's saving power (Rom. 1:16), members who are rooted in Christ (Col. 2:7) and a body which is literally drenched in the Spirit of might and power (1 Cor. 12:13)?

The time has surely come to declare our impatience with contracting, inert churches. Even if the problem is the withholding of divine power, that power is not withheld arbitrarily. God never forsakes His people simply for the fun of it. Nor will he forsake us for the sins of other denominations or of past ages; far less for the sins of the godless society around us. A church which is dying while surrounded by thousands of lost men and women should be asking in all humility, Where have we gone wrong?

Statistics not everything

But what is church growth: *biblical* church growth? Certainly we must insist that statistics are not everything. Other things matter at least as much. It is important, for example, that the quality of individual discipleship should be steadily improving. Far too often people seem to be converted, and that's it. They remain babes, unable to stand strong meat (Heb. 5:12) and demanding that the pulpit (if there is one) keep it simple. Or, to use Paul's figure (Eph. 4:14), they are no better than children, tossed about on the waves of circumstance, from low to high and back again, the prey of every religious charlatan, pursuing 'blessings' to the neglect of ordinary duties and finding them, too often, in nothing more than a new chorus and a good guitarist; or, even more tragically, bewitched by the vestments and mumbo-jumbo of the clergy, by stained-glass windows, the smell of incense and the drama of the Mass.

God doesn't want His people like that. He wants them emotionally stable, content whatever their circumstances (whether abundance or destitution, as Paul put it in Philippians 4:12). We should be growing in knowledge of our Bibles, in our grasp of the great doctrines and in our ability to apply truth in our personal lives. God wants us better and better witnesses, patient sufferers, stronger and stronger in the face of temptation. He wants us to grow in grace, developing, symmetrically, in gentleness and firmness, in meekness and courage, until we have something resembling that true godliness which simultaneously intimidates and attracts.

But God also wants the church to grow in the quality of its collective life. We live in a world divided by barriers of race, class, wealth and education. East and West, North and South, Black and White, Jew and Gentile, live in a state of chronic war, locked into the bitterness of political, economic and social discrimination. The church was meant to be an alternative society. Sadly, it too often duplicates the divisions of the world and many a weary man after a harassing day at the office or on the shop-floor has to face an equally weary evening grappling with his fellow Christians. That is a disgrace. The church is called to reflect the unity of God Himself, its members living face-to-face, pursuing common objectives and sharing together in worship and evangelism. The lack of such fellowship is not occasion simply for Stoical lament, as if we could do nothing about it. It is a summons to *work out* our own salvation (Phil. 2:12) and that is certainly not a matter only of individual piety. It is a matter of our corporate spiritual well-being, requiring us to work at relationships, to crucify individual vanity and power-lust and to encourage co-operation, tolerance and sharing until we arrive at some credible measure of integration and harmony. Only thus can we hope to make a coherent impact on the disorder and despair around us.

But statistics matter too

Yet statistics matter too, as the Book of Acts indicates by so frequently recording the statistical impact of apostolic preaching. At Pentecost there were 3,000 converts and the number quickly rose to 5,000 (Acts 4:4). By the time of Acts 5:14 multitudes were being added to the church, by Acts 6:1 believers were being multiplied, and by Acts 11:21

great numbers were turning to the Lord. The churches in Galatia increased in number daily (Acts 16:5), in Corinth God had 'much people' (Acts 18:10), but at Athens, sadly, the converts were sparse (Acts 17:34). In fact, only a spurious spirituality can be indifferent to numbers. At the beginning of salvation history Abraham was promised a seed as numerous as the sand on the seashore (Gen. 22:17). At its close, the triumphant church of Revelation is 'a great multitude' (Rev. 7:9).

Every Presbyterian minister affirms at his ordination that *zeal for the honour of God, love to Jesus Christ and desire of saving souls* are his great motives and chief inducement for entering upon the work. Such a man can never be indifferent to numbers or to congregational and denominational statistics because he has been called not only to preach but to baptise. His heart longs to bring people to the point of *profession*. Every decline in church attendance or church membership represents a decline in the number of souls being saved, and a man who can take that in his stride should not be in the ministry at all.

But how?

What can we do about church growth? Whatever the importance of revival, biblically and historically, our duty is *reformation*. Revival is no more the total answer to the needs of the church than regeneration is the total answer to the spiritual needs of individuals. God regenerates: we preach. God revives: we reform. God provides the fire from heaven, but we must build up the dilapidated altars (1 Kgs. 18:30).

This is not the place to draw up a complete programme for reformation. But some things are crying out to be done. At one obvious level, it is a case of putting our own house in order. First impressions are enormously important. What impression do our buildings make? Are they cold and tatty?

Are they damp and musty? Is the grass uncut? Have they poor acoustics, not because the problem is insurmountable, but because sentiment insists that things must be left as they were in Dr. So-and-So's day (the Doctor, of course, would soon change them, were he alive today). Is the seating uncomfortable? Is the main auditorium much too large for the congregation, while the poor Sunday School have no decent place to meet?

Man (and woman) is body as well as soul, and it is impossible to listen to the gospel or participate in worship if we are shivering, squirming and unable to hear. A congregation which hasn't painted the gates for thirty years is hardly going to impress a stranger as likely to be zealous in the things of the Spirit. Of course, many congregations are hard-up financially. But many of those that are most hard-up are hanging on to more buildings than they need. Why not sell all but one and make it decent?

And what kind of welcome do visitors receive? Do we give any thought at all to who should be on duty at the church door? Not all are suited to it. Some would be better in the vestry praying. Have those at the door been briefed as to their duty? It is ridiculous how often visitors are left to fend for themselves, wandering bewildered into churches with strange layouts, not knowing where to sit and scared they may sit in a pew which has been in some family for generations. Is it beyond our wit to ensure that they are given a psalmody and a word of explanation, before being courteously shown to a seat?

It would help, too, to have some basic literature which would simultaneously introduce the Church and present the gospel. There is no need for anything elaborate. Local congregations can do it for themselves, explaining the more obvious peculiarities of our worship and setting forth what the Church stands for (which is, one hopes, the Christian gospel).

We must be careful, too, about community relations. Whether we like it or not, our public image often deters people from coming near our churches. But care and wisdom at the local level can go a long way towards overcoming this. Let it be seen that we are interested in the community. If the local people are building a village hall, offer some help from church funds. If local caring groups need a place to meet, offer your premises (church buildings are grossly under-used anyway). If a local asset is being threatened, add your voice to the protest. If the community is agitating for an ante-natal clinic or a proper playground, give your support. Let's take some initiatives of our own as well, such as providing a meeting-point for Old Age Pensioners or a club for the youngsters. Our buildings are invaluable assets. Don't use them only for church services. Use them to meet local needs (and, incidentally, to create goodwill). The only accolade to come our way may be, 'Not your typical Free Church!' But even that may be something, if the prevailing idea of the Church is a caricature.

Discussion
Within the life of every church there must be, somewhere, provision for discussion. This need not (indeed, must not) prejudice stated church services. God knows we need all the straight teaching we can get from called and gifted men. It is no good thing at all to replace preaching with rambling seminars dominated by the most vociferous. But either in a Youth Fellowship or in group Bible Study or in after-church discussion or (best of all) in spontaneous informal gatherings our people need to talk. They need to share experiences, express ideas, ask questions, be contradicted, made to think for themselves and trained to defend their corner. Apart from all else, this is probably the best defence the church has against the excesses of Pentecostalism. When

there is no fellowship, no sharing, no interaction (no kind of body-ministry at all), people are easily persuaded to move in to something that looks warm, friendly and dynamic. Conversely, where there is a true body-life the church can survive anything: even a less than adequate preaching ministry.

The primacy of preaching

But (as everyone's been longing to point out) is it not through the preaching of the gospel that the church is to grow? And are not all these other factors secondary and subordinate? Decidedly so! It does not follow, however, that just because we recognise the primacy of preaching we have nothing to learn in this area. Although there have been many encouraging things in the Church in recent years, it is probably true that the standard of preaching has declined; and certainly true that the number of outstanding preachers is nothing like what it used to be. To many, that will immediately sound dreadfully carnal. But we'll come back to that in a moment.

For example, our preaching has to be aggressive. The Lord did not say merely, Teach! He said, *Go*, teach (Matt. 28:10). We have to put the gospel where the people are, and if they're not in our pews we have to put it somewhere else, using every means available: tracts, press, audio-tapes, videos, songs – anything, in fact, that can express the truth.

For the same reason we have to equip our people to take the gospel into their own spheres of influence. In fact, it should be a major pre-occupation of the pulpit to ensure that ordinary Christians know what they believe, why they believe it, how to express it and how to defend it.

But there is something even more fundamental: Do our pulpits today preach Christ as fully, as freely and as urgently as they did twenty-five years ago? I think not. There is more folksiness and maybe more practical relevance, but there is not as much of Christ and certainly not as much pleading and beseeching. Yet this was the glory of the church in Scotland. This is what distinguished Scottish from Dutch and even from English Calvinism. This is what gave such fragrance to the ministry of Rutherford and Boston and McCheyne. Today, maybe, there is a fear of passion, even in the pulpit. Even more important, today we are less well schooled in our Calvinism, less sure where the boundaries of orthodoxy are and petrified of straying into Arminianism (or a reputation for it). But what kind of Calvinism is this? The Calvinism of Paul (or the Paulinism of Calvin) pleaded with men, as though God Himself were on bended knee (2 Cor. 5:20). The Marrow Men told eighteenth-century Scotland, 'Christ is dead for you! There is salvation for every sinner of mankind lost! Christ is yours to come to! The deed is made out in your name – you have only to take possession!' There is good news for every creature, said the Lord in Mark 16:15. Let's (like John Knox) 'ding the pulpit into blads' telling it.

Does it matter who is in the pulpit?

Finally, to return to the point made above: this whole idea of 'outstanding' preachers, is it not carnal? Does it matter who's in the pulpit? Is not one man as good as any other, provided he has the message?

There is truth in this. The message itself is so stupendous that, provided it is told, the manner of its telling doesn't matter. What are the differences anyway? Aren't we all just earthen vessels? And, in comparison with the message, aren't we all nothing?

But this is by no means the whole truth. We are dealing with human nature and we must never forget that. That nature wearies of the man it hears all the time, even though he be a

Chalmers or a Lloyd-Jones. More important, there are one-talent men and two-talent men. There are also a few five-talent men. Let our people hear great preaching. They will never forget it. Let them have their special services, their conferences, their conventions and their rallies, because human nature needs not only daily bread but annual feasts. Our forefathers had them: their five-day Communion seasons were great feasts. Growing churches all over the world have them, even when their pastors are already great preachers. Our people need them: those weekends, carefully planned and prayed for, when the people gather from near and far to hear a new voice, to be thrilled by a packed church, to be carried up to heaven by melody sung from the heart and, above all, to hear the gospel preached as they have never heard it before.

There are men in the world who can do it. Let our people hear them. And even more, let our young preachers hear them, to give them a taste of real pulpit power and a vision of what's possible when the church is exposed to 'logic on fire'.

7

THE
BASIS
OF
CHRISTIAN UNITY

This chapter first appeared in *Evangel* (Autumn, 1985), pp. 2-11. It is the substance of a lecture delivered at the conference of the British Evangelical Council in 1985.

It is very tempting to regard doctrinal agreement as the basis of Christian unity. We must resist the temptation, however. The basis lies much deeper. The real foundation of our oneness is our common membership of the body of Christ. This, at least, has been the historic Reformed view. Calvin, for example, is clear on it:

> By the unity of the church we must understand a unity into which we feel persuaded that we are truly ingrafted. For unless we are united with all the other members under Christ our Head, no hope of the future inheritance awaits us. All the elect of God are so joined together in Christ that as they depend on one Head, so they are as it were compacted into one body, being knit together like its different members; made truly one by living together under the same Spirit of God in one faith, hope and charity, called not only to the same inheritance of eternal life, but to participation in one God and Christ.[1]

More succinctly, but to the same effect, he writes in the next paragraph:

> For if they are truly persuaded that God is the common Father of them all, and Christ their common Head, they cannot but be united together in brotherly love, and mutually impart their blessings to each other.

Calvin's successors retained this point of view. According to John Owen:

> The Lord Jesus Christ Himself is the original and spring of this union, and every particular church is united to Him as its Head. This relation of the Church unto Christ as its Head, the apostle expressly affirms to be the foundation and cause of its union. Ephesians 4:15, 16; Colossians 2:19. And unless this union be dissolved, unless a church be disunited from Christ, it cannot be so far from the catholic church, nor any true church of Christ in particular, however it may be dealt withal by others in the world.[2]

Charles Hodge wrote in similar vein:

> All Protestants agree that the Church in heaven and on earth is one. There is one fold, one kingdom, one family, one body. They all agree that Christ is the centre of this unity. Believers are one body in Christ Jesus; that is, in virtue of their union with Him.[3]

This is the clear New Testament position: we are one not because of a common polity or a common belief but because we are all Christians. The idea is expressed in a variety of ways. We are all members of the body of Christ (1 Cor. 12:13ff). We are all branches of the vine (John 15:1ff). We are all members of the household of God (Eph. 2:19). We are all fellow-citizens with the saints (Eph. 2:19). We have all been given to Christ (John 17:24), born again by the Spirit (John 3:3), and indwelt by the triune God (John 14:23). We all have God for our Father (1 John 3:1), Christ for our Shepherd (John 10:1ff), and the Holy spirit for our Comforter.

This spiritual unity, an undeniable and irreversible fact, constitutes an unconditional obligation. Because we are united at this level, we owe one another, simply as Christians, recognition, assistance, love and co-operation. We have no right to insist on some other condition. We are one *in Christ*. We may offend against this unity, but we cannot undo it. We only incur the reproach of factiousness and schism.

Nor can we be content with a purely spiritual, ideal, Platonic unity. The believer is not an idea but flesh and blood. The Church is not an idea but flesh and blood. The unity of the Church must have the same visible, concrete reality. This is what the Lord prayed for: 'That they all may be one, that the world may believe that Thou hast sent Me' (John 17:21). The love Christians had for one another was one that the world could see and be impressed by. It became visible in caring for one another (even when they were separated by hundreds of miles, Acts 11:29), by co-operation in evangelism (Phil. 1:5), by public assembly (Heb. 10:25), by mutual consultation (Acts 15:1ff), and by respect for universal practice (1 Cor. 11:33ff). Howard A. Snyder rightly warns against a Platonic dualism which distinguishes between an ideal church (which is safely one) and the real church (which is fragmented, but need not be concerned about it) and goes on to say:

> There is but one people of God on earth, and it is as the people of God that the church is one. This is much more than an invisible spiritual unity. It exists (although imperfectly) in space and time, and for both theological and practical reasons it must be given some structural expression.[4]

Recognising a church

This immediately throws up the problem of recognition. How does one know a Christian or a church when one sees one?

With regard to the former, the surest indication we have is the practice of the apostolic church in connection with baptism. Philip, for example, baptises the Ethiopian on the basis of a very simple profession of faith: 'I believe that Jesus is the Son of God' (Acts 8:37). We know a little more about the 3,000 baptised at Pentecost: they had been convicted by Peter's message, they cried out for spiritual help and they 'gladly received the word'. As such, they were baptised: and afterwards they continued to attend the apostles' instruction, they shared in the fellowship and they participated in the breaking of bread and in the prayers (Acts 2:42).

The most remarkable feature of the apostles' practice is the speed with which they acted in receiving new members. We see this not only in the instances already cited, but also in the cases of Lydia (Acts 16:15), the Jailer (Acts 16:33), and the household of Cornelius (Acts 10:48). There was no period of probation and certainly 'no inquisitorial minuteness' (to quote a phrase from *The Practice of the Free Church of Scotland*). They acted on the judgment of charity. This obviously involved the risk of being wrong and sometimes the apostles *were* wrong: they admitted into the church people whose subsequent conduct showed that they had 'neither part not lot in this matter'. Nor is there any indication within the developing revelation of the New Testament that the apostles ever altered their procedure. To the very end, membership rested on simple profession of faith, judged charitably. The remedy lay not in undue scrutiny at the point of admission but in the application of discipline to unruly members.

Most of us represent so-called 'gathered churches', and this aspect of New Testament teaching should give us pause. 'There's no art to find the mind's construction in the face,' said Shakespeare, and there certainly is no way that church elders can determine a man's spiritual condition from the way he performs in an interview. However great our zeal, we are left judging only 'the outward appearance'. To pretend that one can do more is to make ourselves ridiculous: and to pretend that our churches contain none but saints is to pretend to an insight far exceeding the apostles. In the last analysis, in any tradition, we build the temple with *professed* believers.

But what matters for this paper is not so much how we recognise individual Christians as how we can recognise authentic churches. It was to meet this need that the Reformers developed the doctrine of the so-called marks of the Church. The historical context in which they worked is important. The Reformers were very conscious of the possibility of schism and exceedingly sensitive to the charge that they were guilty of it. This is particularly true of Calvin, who once wrote: 'Those who disrupt from the body of Christ and split its unity into schisms, are quite excluded from the hope of salvation, so long as they remain in dissidence of this kind.'[5] It is not surprising that, holding such a view of the gravity of schisms, he should reply at length to Sadolet's oft-repeated charge that he was 'forsaking the church'. 'It is scarcely possible,' said Calvin, 'that the minds of the common people should not be greatly alienated from you by the many examples of cruelty, avarice, intemperance, annoyance, insolence, lust and all sorts of wickedness, which were openly manifested by men of your order. But,' he adds most significantly, 'none of those things would have driven us to an attempt which we made under a much stronger necessity. This necessity was that the light of divine truth had been extinguished, the Word of God buried, the virtue of Christ left in profound oblivion and the pastoral office subverted.'[6] A little later, he returned to the same theme: 'As to the charge of forsaking the Church, which they are accustomed to bring against me, there is nothing here of which my conscience accuses me, unless indeed he is to be considered a deserter who, seeing the soldiers routed and scattered and abandoning the ranks, raises the leader's standard and recalls them to their post.'[7]

Clearly, Calvin worried about schism. Clearly too, he held that deviations from the norms of Christian conduct did not warrant separation from a professing church. And clearly, above all, he held that the decisive consideration must be adherence to the truth and to the word of God.

It was in this context that Calvin developed his doctrine of the *marks*. He had to rebut the charge of schism: and he had to defend the claim of the Protestants that their churches were real churches.

For Calvin, himself, there were two marks: the ministry of the word and the administration of the sacraments: 'When we say that the pure ministry of the word and pure celebration of the sacraments is a fit pledge and earnest, so that we may safely recognise a church in every society in which both exist, our meaning is, that we are never to discard it so long as these remain, though it may otherwise teem with numerous faults.'[8] But subsequent Reformed theology made significant additions to Calvin's two marks. *The Scots Confession* of 1560 added 'ecclesiastical discipline uprightly administered' (Chap. XVIII). The Westminster Confession added '*public worship* performed, more or less, purely' (Chap. XXV). But the most interesting addition of all was made by the Second Book of Discipline: 'the whole polity of the Church consists in three things, viz. in Doctrine, Discipline and Distribution' (Chap. II). 'Distribution' in this connection means what today would be called the Church's ministry of compassion, the distribution of relief through the diaconate. Its inclusion here is most perceptive.

The result of Reformed reflection over the sixteenth and seventeenth centuries is, then, that five distinct factors enter into the question of ecclesiastical recognition: the preaching of the word, the administration of the sacraments, discipline, public worship, and distribution.

The Preaching of the Word

The danger here is that we may overlook the emphasis on *preaching* the word. It is not the mere possession of the truth and certainly not its encapsulation in a formal constitution that decides the issue, but whether we actually proclaim it. The question being asked at last is whether a church is faithful to the Great Commission: does it go and teach? A church is not a church unless it evangelises. Some years ago, the Reverend Bill Dyer, speaking at the Borders Conference, said that many Reformed churches did no more than pay lip-service to this principle: they put up a church notice advertising the times of their services and saying,

'All welcome!'. 'That,' said Mr. Dyer, 'is like a fisherman putting up a notice to the effect "All fish welcome here!".' We cannot evangelise by attraction. We have to evangelise by aggression, going at the world with the gospel. The mere possession of the word of life is not enough. We have to hold it forth (Phil. 2:16).

The converse of this is that a church may have a defective constitution and yet preach the gospel. To take one example: the current effective constitution of the Church of Scotland is theologically minimal. While giving a courteous nod to the Westminster Confession, in practice the Church is bound to nothing except the doctrine of the Trinity and 'the Scottish Reformation'. Because there is no standard of theology, the most bewildering theological pluralism prevails. The constitution does not safeguard the gospel. Yet, there is no denying that the gospel is preached: fully and brilliantly in some pulpits, adequately in others, minimally in yet others (and probably not at all in some).

In any judgment of a church then, we have to look beyond its actual constitution. Some with admirable constitutions do nothing by way of evangelism; while others, with radically defective constitutions, do a great deal. The question is whether the church in the totality of its life, communicates and expresses the gospel.

Obviously there can never be complete doctrinal agreement among Christians. No two believers will be unanimous on the whole range of their beliefs. It was for this reason that while the Reformers and their successors laid such emphasis on doctrine as a mark of a true church, they were careful not to insist on too wide an area of agreement. A man like Burroughs, for example, was anxious that 'articles should be as few as may be,' while Cradock ascribed much of the fragmentation of the church to an over-scrupulous orthodoxy: 'There will never be peace among the saints as long as every one stands so firm on his points and will not abate an ace.'[9]

What these men were pleading for was a sense of theological proportion. Some doctrines were fundamental and some were not. Some were primary and some were secondary.

This distinction was clearly drawn by the Second Vatican Council: 'Catholic theologians, in comparing doctrines, should bear in mind that there is an order or hierarchy of the truths of Catholic doctrine, since these truths are variously linked up with the foundation of the Christian faith. All doctrines are equally necessary. But they are not all equally important.'[10]

However, this distinction was a commonplace of Reformed theology, centuries before Vatican II. It goes back at least as far as John Calvin, who said bluntly, 'All the heads of true doctrine are not in the same position.'[11] In the following chapter, he speaks of certain errors in the ministry of the word and sacraments as 'trivial', and goes on to define precisely what he means: 'There are errors by which the fundamental doctrine of religion is not injured, and by which these articles of religion, in which all believers should agree, are not suppressed.'

The Church dies only when 'falsehood has forced its way into the citadel of religion and the sum of necessary doctrine is inverted'.[12]

So far as Calvin was concerned, a church could retain a pure ministry of the word and yet 'otherwise teem with numerous faults'. He writes:

> Nay, even in the administration of word and sacraments defects may creep in which ought not to alienate us from its communion. For all the heads of true doctrine are not in the same position. Some are so necessary to be known that all must hold them to be fixed and undoubted as the proper credentials of religion: for instance, that God is one, that Christ is God, and the Son of God,

that our salvation depends on the mercy of God, and the like. Others again, which are the subject of controversy among the churches, do not destroy the unity of the faith. For why should it be regarded as a ground of dissension between churches, if one, without any spirit of contention or perverseness in dogmatising, hold that the soul, in quitting the body, flies to heaven, and another, without venturing to speak positively as to the abode, holds it for certain that it lives with the Lord? A difference of opinion as to these matters which are not absolutely necessary ought not to be a ground of dissension among Christians. The best thing, indeed, is to be perfectly agreed, but seeing there is no man who is not involved in the mists of ignorance, we must either have no church at all, or pardon delusion in those things of which we may be ignorant, without violating the substance of religion, and forfeiting salvation. Here, however, I have no wish to patronise even minutest errors, as if I thought it right to foster them by flattery or connivance: what I say is, that we are not on account of every minute difference to abandon a church, provided it retains sound and unimpaired that doctrine in which the safety of piety consists, and keeps the rite of the sacraments instituted by the Lord. Meanwhile, if we strive to reform what is offensive, we act in the discharge of duty.[13]

The theologians of the seventeenth century accepted Calvin's distinction unreservedly and applied it vigorously against the schismatics of their own day. Rutherford, for example, defended the separation from Rome on the very same ground as the Reformer: 'though they profess the true God, as Edom did, *yet they clearly evert the fundamentals.*' He went on to say, 'If a preacher be sound in the main, though he mix errors with his teaching, you may sit under his ministry.'[14]

John Owen differed from Rutherford on many things, not least on church polity. But he fully accepted the distinction between fundamental and non-fundamental doctrines. In his classic work, *On the True Nature of a Gospel Church*, for example, he asks 'whether a man may be excommunicated for errors in matters of faith, or false opinions about them' and answers: 'If the errors intended are about or against the *fundamental truths* of the gospel, so as that they that hold them cannot "hold the Head" but really "make shipwreck of the faith", no pretended usefulness of such persons nor peaceableness as unto outward deportment, can countenance the church in forbearing, after due admonition, to cut them off from their communion.'[15] A few lines later, he adds, 'False opinions in lesser things, when the foundation of faith and Christian practice is not immediately concerned, may be tolerated in a church.'

Probably the fullest exposition of this distinction is to be found in the work of the nineteenth-century Scottish theologian, William Cunningham. Cunningham lays down the general principle that, 'There is a great difference in point of intrinsic importance among the many truths of different classes taught in Scripture.'[16] The general measure of a doctrine's importance, he says, is its relation to the leading object of revelation, which is to make known the ruin and recovery of mankind.

Cunningham applies this distinction in four different directions.

First, in relation to Roman Catholicism: 'It is manifestly impossible to unravel the sophistries and to answer the arguments of Papists on the subject of the unity of the church without admitting or assuming the existence of a distinction in point of intrinsic importance among the articles of revealed truth – a distinction commonly expressed by saying that some are fundamental and some are not.'[17] Those who hold to these fundamental doctrines belong to the one church of Christ, even though they live outwith the communion of Rome.

Secondly, Cunningham applied the distinction in evaluating Socinianism. The churches have held themselves fully warranted in denying the Socinians the name and character of Christians on the ground that, 'Socinianism is a deliberate and determined rejection of *the whole substance of the message* which Christ and His apostles conveyed from God to man.'[18]

Thirdly, he applied the distinction in assessing the Pelagian controversy and came to what by today's standards would be a remarkable conclusion: 'The history of the church seems to indicate that somehow the prosperity of vital religion is more clearly connected with correct views of the points involved in the Pelagian controversy than even with correct views upon the subject of the Trinity and of the person of Christ.'[19]

Fourthly, Cunningham applied the distinction between fundamental and non-fundamental doctrines when he came to assessing the relative importance of the Arminian controversy. This is probably the area where Reformed churchmen are most liable to lose a sense of proportion. Cunningham supplies a useful corrective: 'In the scheme of Christian theology,' he writes, 'there is a class of doctrines which may be said to occupy a higher platform than what are commonly called the distinctives of Calvinism.'[20] Specifically, these are the doctrines which Calvinists have in common with orthodox Lutherans and evangelical Arminians: human depravity, the deity and humanity of Christ, the atonement, the Spirit's agency in regeneration and sanctification. 'Those who agree with us in holding Scriptural views on these points, while they reject the peculiar doctrines of Calvinism,' writes Cunningham, 'agree with us on subjects that are more important and fundamental and that ought to occupy a more prominent place in the ordinary course of pulpit instruction than those in which they differ from us.'

Cunningham was conscious, of course, that Calvinists had not always retained a biblical sense of proportion in connection with their favourite doctrines. 'There can be no reasonable doubt,' he comments, 'that the peculiarities of Calvinism were raised for a time to a position of undue prominence and that there are plain indications of this in some of the features of the theological literature of the 17th century.' 'We have the highest sense,' he continues, 'of the value for many important purposes, of these theological systems. But we cannot doubt that Calvin's *Institutes* is fitted to leave upon the mind a juster and sounder impression of the place which the doctrines of Calvinism hold in the Bible, and ought to hold permanently in the usual course of the pulpit instruction, or in the ordinary preaching of the gospel.'[21]

Or, we might add, in whatever is to serve as the basis of Christian unity.

A word of caution is necessary, however. George Gillespie rightly warns against equating fundamental doctrines with 'the first rudiments, or A.B.C. of a catechism, which we first of all put to new beginners'. 'Heresy,' he writes, 'is not to be so far restricted as that no error shall be accounted heretical but that which is destructive to some fundamental of the Christian faith: if by a fundamental article you understand such a truth without the knowledge and faith of which it is impossible to get salvation.'[22] How much did any of us know, consciously, and articulately, in the first moment of faith in Christ? How much did Lydia know when she was baptised? Or the Philippian Jailer (Acts 16:15, 33) or Naaman (2 Kgs 5:15)? At the commencement of our own Christian lives, we are, all of us, ignorant of some fundamental doctrines.

A doctrinal basis of union between churches cannot be levelled to the capacity of spiritual infants. It is impossible to answer the question, how much must a human being know before we can judge him to be in a state of salvation? The real question, in the language of the Westminster Confession, is, how much must be known for God's glory, man's salvation, faith and life? (Chap. I.VI). In this form of words, the meaning of salvation is not restricted to conversion. It includes the whole experience of salvation, including sanctification and the life of faith. The fundamental doctrines are those without which we cannot live to the glory of God, come to maturity in faith, experience biblical sanctification or live lives of obedience.

Identifying fundamental doctrines

But how are we to identify them?

First, they are the doctrines 'so clearly propounded and opened in some place of Scripture or other that not only the learned but the unlearned, in a due use of the ordinary means, may attain unto a sufficient understanding of them'.[23] The assumption here is that whatever the ambiguity of Scripture on some peripheral matters, it will speak with unmistakable clarity on the fundamentals: and this will be reflected in the unanimity of the Lord's people on these issues. These doctrines are already clear for the most part in the Old Testament and figure prominently in the message which Paul brought before the Areopagus (Acts 17:1ff). They include the unity, spirituality, holiness and graciousness of God: the doctrines of creation and providence; the affirmation of man as a creature made by God in His own image but now fallen and depraved; and the doctrine of man's accountability at a final reckoning.

Secondly, there are doctrines which the New Testament specifically affirms to be fundamental. The most important passage in this connection is 1 Corinthians 15:3-5: 'For I delivered to you as of first importance what I also received, that Christ died for our sins in accordance with the Scriptures, that He was buried, that He rose on the third day according to the Scripture and that He appeared to Cephas, then to the twelve.' Behind the words, 'as of first importance', there lies the Greek phrase *en protois*, literally 'among the first things'. This is itself a clear recognition of a distinction between matters of primary importance and matters of only secondary importance. Among the primary and fundamental things are, for Paul, the authority of Scripture, the doctrine of vicarious, sacrificial atonement and the resurrection of Christ. These things stood in the forefront of the evangelistic message.

Another interesting passage is Galatians 1:8: 'If we, or an angel from heaven, should preach to you a gospel contrary to that which we preached to you, let him be accursed.' If certain elements in the message are tampered with, then the gospel ceases to be a gospel (verse 7). What these elements are is clear from the Epistle as a whole: justification has its source in the grace of God, its ground in the work of Christ, and the only contribution we make to it is to believe. Justification by faith alone, in other words, is fundamental. To abandon it is to desert Christ and turn to an alien religion.

The fundamental status of the resurrection of Christ is emphasised again in 1 Corinthians 15:14: 'If Christ has not been raised, then our preaching is in vain and your faith is in vain.' Paul obviously has in mind a literal resurrection (a resurrection of the flesh) because its proof is that Christ was *seen* (verses 5 and 6). If that doctrine is not true, says the Apostle, then Christian faith is a pathetic waste of time.

In 2 Timothy 2:17, it is not the resurrection of Christ but the resurrection of believers (and possibly, of all men) that is in view. Hymenaeus and Philetus have subverted this doctrine not by denying it outright but by spiritualising it. According to them, the resurrection has already taken place. Paul reacts passionately. Such teaching is tantamount to turning away from the truth itself. It eats away at faith like a gangrene. It attacks the very foundation on which the Church is built.

Turning very briefly to the question of Christology, we note two crucial passages. One is Peter's confession at Caesarea Philippi, 'You are the Christ, the Son of the Living God' (Matt. 16:16). This confession, asserting both the Messiahship and the deity of Christ, is the rock on which the Church is built. Apart from it, worship of Christ is pure idolatry.

The other passage is 1 John 4:2-3: 'Every spirit which confesses that Jesus Christ has come in the flesh is of God: every spirit which does not confess Jesus is not of God. This is the spirit of antichrist.' It is a curiosity of the history of doctrine that the first major Christological heresy should be Docetism, with its denial of the humanness of Christ. To deny that humanness, that flesh, is heresy, says John. Today this is something that we are inclined to forget, imagining that in the desperate struggle to defend the Saviour's deity we must concede as little as possible to His humanity. 'Scarcely any of us in Scotland,' lamented Dr. John Duncan, 'give due prominence to the Incarnation.'[24]

The third category of fundamental doctrines consists of those that are enshrined in the great creeds of the Church. These overlap largely with those asserted by Scripture itself to be primary. Or, to express it otherwise, they represent the doctrines believed by all Christians, always and everywhere. The most universal and comprehensive of these is the Apostles' Creed, a summary of basic beliefs going back to the fourth century. This summary includes: the fatherhood of God, His almightiness as Creator, the divine sonship of Christ, His virgin birth, His crucifixion, death and burial, His resurrection and ascension, His second coming, the unity, holiness and catholicity of the Church, the resurrection of the body and the life everlasting.

The later creeds gave sharp focus to crucial doctrines as these providentially became subjects of acute controversy and thorough investigation. The Nicene Creed focused particularly on the deity of Christ, giving it precise expression in the word *homoousios*: Christ is one and the same in being with God the Father. The later Nicaeno/Constantinopolitan Creed made the same claim for the Holy Spirit. The Athanasian Creed gathered the specific assertions of these two earlier ones into a comprehensive statement of the doctrine of the Trinity. The Formula of Chalcedon (451 AD) gave dogmatic formulation to the Church's primary Christological convictions: Christ is true God, Christ is true man, Christ is one person. The Reformation Creeds asserted the gospel over against the semi-Pelagianism of Rome, giving belated formal expression to the distinctive theology of Augustine. These creeds proclaimed the total (pervasive) depravity of man, and the necessity and actuality of salvation by grace.

There is then a threefold approach to the problem of ascertaining fundamental doctrines: what doctrines are revealed in Scripture with such clarity that all Christians are agreed on them? what doctrines does Scripture itself describe as fundamental? and what doctrines has the Church sought to define and safeguard in its great creeds?

Having asked these questions, the first thing that strikes us is how long the list of fundamental doctrines actually is:

1. *The unity, spirituality, personalness, holiness and graciousness of God.*

2. *The doctrine of creation: especially the creation of man in the image of God.*

3. *The fall, and the depravity, of man.*

4. *Man's accountability to God at a final judgment.*

5. *The authority of the Scriptures.*

6. *Vicarious atonement by the sacrifice of Christ.*

7.   *The resurrection of Christ.*
8.   *Justification by faith alone.*
9.   *The resurrection of the body.*
10.   *The consubstantial deity of Christ.*
11.   *The true and perfect humanity of Christ.*
12.   *The virgin birth of Christ.*
13.   *The ascension.*
14.   *The second coming.*
15.   *The Church as a divine institution, marked by unity, holiness and universality.*
16.   *The consubstantial deity and authentic personalness of the Holy Spirit.*
17.   *The fatherhood of God.*
18.   *The life everlasting.*

When we consider that the Westminster Confession, often criticised for inordinate length, has only thirty-three chapters, ten of which deal with matters relating to the Church, the sacraments and the civil power, it is astonishing that even a cursory examination of first principles should yield eighteen fundamental articles. The plea for a minimal confession (for example: 'Jesus Christ is Lord!') clearly cannot claim the support of Scripture.

The second intriguing fact is that, so far as doctrine is concerned, there really is a surprising unanimity among Christians. As Charles Hodge points out, 'It is far greater than would be inferred from the contentions of theologians, and it includes everything essential to Christianity.'[25] In fact, in many instances, it would be hypocrisy to claim that our divisions had anything to do with doctrinal considerations at all. Many of them have been the result of differences of opinion on matters of Church government, worship and discipline: of disputes on baptism, exclusive psalmody, and relations with the state. Too many churches are split-offs from other churches and owe their existence to nothing more honourable than clashes of personality.

Thirdly, in many of the instances when doctrinal considerations have entered into the calculations, the doctrines concerned have been relatively unimportant. Some churches have split over the millennium, others over the role of the civil magistrate in religion and yet others on the issue of common grace. No one with any sense of theological proportion can defend such separations. Reformed theologians have never been unanimous on these questions, any more than they have dogmatised on the infra-supra-lapsarian controversy or the length of the days of Genesis. Dabney differed from Hodge on some questions relating to the imputation of Adam's sin; and Owen disagreed with Rutherford on whether retributive justice was essential or discretionary in God. In these intra-confessional (as distinct from inter-confessional) disputes, men held their views firmly and argued them passionately. But they would not set up separate churches.

Fourthly, it seems clear, on any realistic scale of theological values, that the points of difference between evangelicals and Roman Catholics are not as important as those between evangelicals and Socinians (and their modern counterparts, so-called radical theologians of all hues). Because of history, the reaction of Evangelicals to Roman Catholicism is often irrational and sometimes even hysterical. Yet, so far as fundamental doctrines are concerned, Socinianism was much more dangerous. It denied the authority of Scripture, the deity of Christ, the trinity and the atonement. Their modern counterparts do the same and even carry the assault further. The advocates of demythologization argue that we can now know virtually nothing of the life and teaching of Christ. Others spiritualise the resurrection, just like Hymenaeus and Philetus. Yet others deny the immortality of the soul. Most modern theologians deny the doctrine of a historic Fall (and thus accept implicitly the Manichean doctrine that God *made* man evil). And at the farthest extreme, some, while professing to be Christians, deny the existence of a personal God.

Yet to many Christians, the Pope is more damnable than Don Cupitt. This is irrational. According to the Apostle John, the antichrist is the one who denies the incarnation. Yet in the whole range of Christological dogmas, Rome has stood firm: in fact the Formula of Chalcedon, that bulwark of orthodoxy, reflects, substantially, the famous *Tome* of Pope Leo the Great (400-461).

The sentiments of Dr. John Duncan on this whole question are worth pondering. 'Very many Protestants,' he once said, 'are Nestorian without knowing it. It is not so with the Catholics. You will never find a Roman priest wandering from the Catholic faith on the person of Christ, or in reference to the Trinity.'[26] When asked, 'How do you account for that?', Duncan replied: 'It is probably because the idler Protestants have engrossed themselves with the one doctrine of justification, and made it bulk too largely, forgetting its foundation. There are fundamentals beneath justification. The person of Christ is fundamental. Justification by faith is the meeting-point of many doctrines, a rallying centre of theology; but it is not the foundation doctrine.'

Since Duncan's day, of course, things have changed. Vatican II represents a Catholic ethos radically more evangelical than Vatican I (an ethos which the hierarchy appears to be currently in process of rejecting): and Roman Catholic scholars, such as Hans Küng and Edward Schillebeeckx have both advocated Christologies which blatantly contradict Catholic orthodoxy. Yet the papacy has dealt far more firmly with these deviants than have the Protestant authorities with John Hick, Maurice Wiles, James P. Mackay and G. W. H. Lampe.[28] Certainly, the Church of Rome would not qualify for the rebuke addressed to his own denomination by G. E. Duffield: 'We must face the serious implications of the fact that clerical assent to the Thirty-Nine Articles has, during the past century, been so devalued as now to be almost meaningless, and that all idea of doctrinal discipline within the Church of England seems to be abandoned.'[29] While evangelicals have either marshalled their forces at the frontiers with (16th century) Catholicism, or fought various civil wars among themselves, little has been done to defend the citadel: 'Jesus Christ *Himself* being the chief corner-stone' (Eph. 2:20).

The functions of creeds

As we have seen, many of the fundamental doctrines of Christianity have been expressed in the great creeds of the Church. But subscription to these creeds should be imposed only on the Church's officebearers. This goes back to the New Testament itself where the criteria applied to baptisands are clearly not the same as those applied to ordinands. The Church baptised novices. But it would not ordain them (1 Tim. 3:6). Those being baptised professed only, 'Jesus is Lord!' or, 'Jesus is the Son of God!' But deacons 'must hold the mystery of the faith with pure conscience' (1 Tim. 3:9). The presbyter/bishop must be 'apt to teach' (1 Tim. 3:2) and 'hold firm to the sure word as taught, so that he may be able to give instruction in sound doctrine and also to confute those who contradict it' (Titus 1:9). The existence of some form of creed for teachers is clearly hinted at in the words of Paul to Timothy: 'Follow the pattern of the sound words which you have heard from me, in the faith and love which are in Christ Jesus' (2 Tim. 1:13).

Such creeds have a threefold function.

First, they serve as *confessions* in which particular churches or denominations announce to others and to the world their understanding of Christianity. It may be argued, of course, that 'the Bible, the Bible, alone, is the religion of Protestants'. But sometimes we must face the question, 'Yes, but how do you understand the Bible?' and give our answer in the form of a succinct statement of our beliefs with regard to the main articles of religion. At this level, the publication of a creed is simply one form of the Church's preaching.

Secondly, creeds are *standards* of orthodoxy. This is particularly true of the shorter creeds, such as the Nicene, which deal not with the broad spectrum of Christian truths but with a limited number of disputed and controverted points (for example, the deity of Christ). The formulators of the Nicene Creed made no attempt to give a balanced account of Christianity. They simply wanted to draft a statement on the deity of Christ which no Arian or semi-Arian could sign. The later Reformation creeds contained a good deal of non-controversial matter on such topics as effectual calling, adoption and sanctification, but even they were drafted with the conscious intention of excluding from the ministry those who held to the heretical teaching of Arius, Apollinarius, Nestorius, Eutyches, Rome, Socinus and Arminius. Were we drafting such standards today, we would consider further exclusions – for example, Darwinism, Kenoticism and, possibly, Pentecostalism. At this point we have to bear in mind that just as not all truths are fundamental, so not all errors are heresies.

Thirdly, creeds serve as *symbols* of union (which is why the specialised study of creeds is sometimes called *symbolics*). Even as standards they had this function: heresy has to be excluded because it divides. The creeds defined the limits of theological pluralism. Positively, they indicated the area of doctrinal agreement between particular

Christians. Nicea, Chalcedon and Westminster all declared: 'These are the doctrines on which we are all agreed.' Obviously, the larger the number of such doctrines the better: a church has no real unity if all it can confess corporately is 'Jesus is Lord!' On the other hand, to extend the number of doctrines in a symbol beyond the range of the fundamentals is to run the risk of shedding many true believers who do not see some esoteric points of truth exactly as we do. Other things being equal, it is better to leave a doctrine an open question than to exclude a brother from the fellowship.

Pentecostalism

There is one final issue to be faced in connection with the function of doctrine as a mark of the Church. Where do the peculiar doctrines of Pentecostalism and neo-Pentecostalism stand on the theological scale? This is an area where we cannot appeal to the past. We must do our own thinking.

It is important to make some distinctions here. Tongue-speaking is not itself a decisive criterion. So far as we can see, it was not intended to be permanent; it disappeared from the Church for centuries and it would now be impossible to identify it with any certainty. On the other hand, the early believers did speak in tongues and it would be unwarranted to make the mere practice of this 'gift' a basis for exclusion.

The real problem lies in two other areas: Holy Spirit baptism and prophesying. Union with Pentecostals would involve having these doctrines imposed on us as fundamentals and this is an imposition we simply could not accept. The view that Holy Spirit baptism is restricted to certain believers is hardly asserted in Scripture to be fundamental, nor is it revealed repeatedly and unambiguously, nor is it one on which all Christians have been agreed. In fact, it is in its very nature anti-evangelical, implying that we can be believers, and be in Christ, and still lack the very promise of God. When we are told, in addition, that it is something that we must earn (by whatever process) we are back in pure legalism.

So far as prophecy is concerned, much depends on how it is defined: if prophets are simply expositors under another name, there is no problem. But if their pretended role is to deliver special revelations, their claims are an outright challenge to the Protestant view of Scripture, according to which nothing is to be added to the Bible 'whether by new revelations of the Spirit or traditions of men'.[30]

We should note carefully the precise logic of this situation. The question is not whether Pentecostal views on prophecy and Spirit baptism constitute grounds for separation: but whether these views are fundamental and should be safeguarded in any basis of union. Pentecostals would insist that they are fundamental and that they should be safeguarded. I personally find the doctrine of a subsequent Spirit baptism as unacceptable as the doctrine of purgatory: and the ministry of a prophet as repellent as that of a priest.

The Sacraments

The second mark of the Church is the administration of the sacraments according to the will of Christ. Where there are no sacraments there is no Church. The two sacraments, baptism and the Lord's Supper, raise different issues and require separate treatment.

The Lord's Supper

Unity around the Lord's Supper involves three factors. First, agreement as to the elements or symbols used. The Lord, in instituting this sacrament, used bread and wine. Many, probably even most, evangelicals today, use unfermented grape juice. This is not a matter of mere convenience or taste on their part. They object in principle to the use of alcohol. Many of us, however, find this scrupulosity deeply disturbing. It not only involves a clear departure from biblical precedent, but implies adverse criticism of the wisdom and integrity of our Lord. The sacrament is not administered according to the mind of Christ if it wilfully departs from His example.

Secondly, agreement as to the celebrant. In Catholicism, it is insisted that only a priest, duly ordained in the apostolic succession, can preside at the sacrament and pronounce the words of consecration. Even the Westminster Confession allowed itself to say that neither sacrament might 'be administered by any, but by a minister of the word lawfully ordained' (Chap. XXVII. IV). By this standard, the Lord's Supper, as administered in many of the free churches, is at least irregular and possibly invalid. On the other hand, it is very doubtful whether such concepts as 'administering the sacraments' and 'lawful ordination' have any meaning by New Testament standards. All that is necessary is that the sacrament be administered 'decently and in order'.

Thirdly, there must be basic agreement as to the nature of the sacrament itself. Current Roman Catholic thought (or at least Vatican II thought) proposes an ecclesiology which is basically sacramental. A group of believers is a church if it has 'the substance of the eucharistic mystery': *ubi eucharistia ibi ecclesia* (where there is the eucharist, there is the church). Yet the Roman Catholic understanding of this sacrament is such that those of Reformed persuasion would find it impossible to engage in any form of joint participation. (Roman Catholicism is equally conscious of the difficulties from its own side. This is why Vatican II's *Decree on Ecumenism* discourages 'worship in common', making the enigmatic statement, 'The expression of unity very generally forbids common worship.')

Many evangelicals would, of course, recoil instinctively from the idea of participating in Holy Communion according to the Roman form. But that does not absolve us from the responsibility of knowing the theological basis of our objection. There are three main difficulties:

1. The question of the *real presence*. This phrase is sometimes used even by Reformed evangelicals but it should be borne in mind that *real* here has its strict etymological meaning: *real* presence is the presence of the *res* (Latin for *thing*). It means the presence of *the thing itself*, the thing being, in this instance, the body of Christ. In traditional Roman Catholic theology, this presence of the body is asserted literally. The words of consecration by the officiating priest effect a transubstantiation so that the whole substance of the bread is transformed into the whole substance of Christ: body, soul and divinity. To participate in the Mass is to associate wilfully with this doctrine. Despite obvious embarrassment on traditional terminology and elucidation, there is no sign of this doctrine being abated. *The Final Report* of the Anglican-Roman Catholic International Commission, written in as eirenic a tone as possible, is still declaring: 'The elements are not mere signs; Christ's body and blood become really present and are really given' (III 9).

2. The understanding of the Mass as a propitiatory sacrifice. This is a clear element in the theology of the Council of Trent: 'Forasmuch as in this divine sacrifice which is celebrated in the Mass, that same Christ is contained and immolated in an unbloody manner who once offered himself in a bloody manner on the altar of the cross: the holy Synod teaches that this sacrifice is truly propitiatory, and that by means thereof this is effected, that we obtain mercy.'[31]

More recently, those theologians influenced by Vatican II have shown an inclination not only to mute this emphasis but to subject it to radical re-interpretation. To quote *The Final Report* again: 'Christ's death on the cross, the culmination of his whole life of obedience, was the one, perfect and sufficient sacrifice for the sins of the world. There can be no repetition of, or addition to what was then accomplished once for all by Christ. Any attempt to express a nexus between the sacrifice of Christ and the Eucharist must not obscure this fundamental fact of the Christian faith.'[32] Those sentiments are welcome. Nevertheless the formulations of Trent remain the official Catholic position and probably reflect grassroots opinion far more accurately than the words of the conciliators.

3. The adoration of the host (the *host* being in this case the *hostia* [sacrifice]). 'In the holy sacrament of the Eucharist, Christ, the only-begotten Son of God, is to be adored with the worship, even external, of *latria*: and is to be venerated with special festive solemnity and solemnly borne about in procession.'[33] (*Latria* is worship in the highest possible sense.)

This is a perfectly logical practice if the doctrine of transubstantiation is correct, because the bread is now God. However, if the bread has not been transubstantiated, it remains bread and any worship offered to it is idolatry.

The Roman Catholic doctrine has been massively influential, especially in connection with the question of Christ's presence in the Lord's Supper. Let us look briefly at three examples of this influence.

1. **The recent Report,** *Baptism, Eucharist and Ministry*, **published by the Faith and Order Commission of the World Council of Churches**. This document appears to accept unequivocally a literal interpretation of the words, 'This is my body.' What Christ declared is true, and this truth is fulfilled every time the Eucharist is celebrated. The church

confesses Christ's real, living and active presence in the eucharist. The presence of Christ is clearly the centre of the eucharist, and the promise contained in the words of *institution* is therefore fundamental to the celebration.[34] Clearly, the eucharistic theology of mainline ecumenism is going to have a strong Roman flavour.

2. **The Doctrine of Martin Luther**. Luther too, took his stand on a literal interpretation of the words, 'This is my body.' This led to an inevitable insistence on the presence of Christ's body in the Sacrament and to the eventual development within Lutheranism of the doctrine of *consubstantiation* (a word Luther himself did not use). The only difference between this and transubstantiation was that, whereas in the latter the bread and wine ceased to exist (leaving only the substance of Christ), in the Lutheran doctrine the bread and wine continued to exist and the body and blood of Christ were present 'in, with and under' them. In Lutheranism, of course, the doctrine of the presence was not linked with any idea of propitiatory sacrifice, or with the practice of adoring the host. It had, however, profound implications for Christology – every Lord's Day, the body of Christ had to be in thousands of different places at once. This required a doctrine of the ubiquity of the Lord's human nature, arrived at, in turn, by a doctrine of the *communicatio idiomatum* which was peculiarly Lutheran.[35]

Luther's insistence on his doctrine of the corporeal presence of Christ in the Eucharist tragically split the Reformation movement. Today, the question is still with us: Does the doctrine of consubstantiation represent such a radical distortion of the biblical teaching as to make it impossible for the Reformed to participate in the Lutheran sacrament?

3. **The teaching of John Calvin**. Calvin never really shook off the legacy of the mediaeval doctrine. He continued to insist on a certain presence of the body of Christ, and a certain influence emanating from that body. The result, according to William Cunningham, was a doctrine which was 'about as unintelligible as Luther's consubstantiation'.[36] Few Reformed theologians, however, have analysed Calvin's doctrine as carefully as Cunningham and many have accepted it uncritically, continuing to speak of a real presence and to protest loudly against so-called Zwinglianism and the doctrine that the sacraments are only 'naked and bare signs'. Calvin's doctrine of the presence of Christ in the Lord's Supper must never become an article of faith or a term of communion.

So far as the New Testament is concerned, the Lord's Supper is duly administered when we seek to fulfil the fourfold intention of the Lord: to give thanks for God's salvation in Him; to commemorate Him: to proclaim Him; and to have communion with Him and His people.

The question of the Lord's presence in the Sacrament is not raised by the New Testament material itself. Once it is raised, however, we have to say two things, both of them negative: first, that the *body* of Christ is not present in any sense; and, secondly, that the Lord is not present at the Lord's Supper in any *unique* sense. He indwells His people always. He is present with those gathered in His name always. He is present to faith always. He is present in baptism, in preaching and in prayer as really as He is in Holy Communion.

Baptism
On the face of things, every baptised person should recognise every other baptised person as a Christian. But the situation is complicated by several factors.

First, it is complicated by the doctrine of baptismal regeneration, according to which the mere administration and reception of the sacrament regenerates. This doctrine is so radically anti-evangelical that any basis of union would have to specifically exclude it, using some form of words such as those of the Westminster Confession: 'grace and salvation are not so inseparably annexed unto this ordinance as that all that are baptised are undoubtedly regenerated' (Chapter XXVIII, V).

Secondly, there is the question of the *mode* of baptism. Anglicans and Presbyterians regard the mode as immaterial: it may be by sprinkling, by pouring or by immersion. Baptists insist that it must be by immersion and regard any other mode as invalid.

Thirdly, the problem of the subjects of baptism. Anglicans and Presbyterians baptise not only believers but the children of believers. Baptists baptise believers only and regard infant baptism as invalid.

There is no hope of this dispute being resolved. Anglicans and Presbyterians may as well recognise that 'you shall have the Baptists with you always'. Nor is it possible to gather the two views into one church. If only the mode were in dispute, union might be possible, provided paedobaptists were prepared to accept immersion for the sake of peace (whether they would have a right to sacrifice their freedom in this way is a moot point). But the prevalence of two views as to *who* should be baptised makes organic union impossible. However flexible paedobaptists might be with regard to immersion, they could not abandon the practice of infant-baptism, which they regard as a divine institution. So long as this difference remains, the existence of separate evangelical churches side by side will be a painful and humiliating necessity.

Besides pleading for mutual respect, frequent consultation, co-operation in witness and fellowship in prayer, we may make two special pleas.

First, that baptists think carefully about the implications of re-baptism. When these things are done remotely and anonymously there is only a minimum of pain. But I would find it impossible to have fellowship with a church which insisted on re-baptising members of my own. The act is fundamentally schismatic because it says that paedobaptist churches are not valid churches and paedobaptist ministers are not valid ministers (how can a man be 'ordained' before he is baptised?). The correct course would be for baptist churches to recognise that if the rest of us baptise infants, then *we* shall answer to God. Otherwise, they must accept that every baptism of unbelievers (including, surely, many baptists) is invalid; and, more painfully, that they can have meaningful ecumenical relations only with other baptists churches.

The other plea is that paedobaptists abandon the practice of indiscriminate baptism. We have no right to baptise the children of any but believers, and baptists are fully justified in regarding the current practice of many Presbyterians and Anglicans as deeply offensive.

The remaining marks of the Church (discipline, distribution and worship) can be dealt with only cursorily.

Discipline

This must not be restricted to what is referred to today as 'church discipline'. The Scottish Second Book of Discipline, for example, is subtitled, 'Heads and Conclusions of the Polity of the Church.' When the Reformers and their successors spoke of discipline as a mark of the Church, this is clearly what they had in mind. A true church would have a biblical polity.

Discussion as to what constitutes such a polity is often bedevilled by debate as to the meaning of *office, ordination* and such technical terms as *elder, bishop, deacon* and *evangelist.* It is doubtful if these terms were ever used with the precision our western minds long for: and certain that each separate word does not designate a separate office. It is much more fruitful to ask what ministries the apostolic church was furnished with. The answer appears to be, Three: a ministry of tables (deacons, male and female); a ministry of oversight (pastors, bishops, elders); and a ministry of the word. This last can itself be viewed under two aspects: a ministry of the word for the instruction and edification of the church; and a ministry of the word directed, through aggressive evangelism, to making disciples of all nations. There is no hint, however, that these two forms of word-ministry, although conceptually distinct, involved two separate 'offices'. What matters is that any basis of union will have to make provision for all these forms of ministry. The nomenclature is not important.

Independents and Presbyterians would both argue that at least the main features of their respective polities are laid down in the New Testament. But today neither claims divine right for its own discipline. At least they do not dismiss other bodies as mere sects on the ground of differences in church government. Nor would they insist on the re-ordination of ministers admitted from other communions: or even on a service of reconciliation.

Anglicans and Roman Catholics, however, see things differently. Romanists have serious reservations about Anglican orders and Anglicans have serious reservations about the orders of the free churches. Even an eclectic, ecumenical document such as the *Report on Baptism, Eucharist and Ministry* clearly expects any future ecclesiastical alignments to be episcopal. 'The threefold ministry', it says, 'of bishop, presbyter and deacon may serve today as an expression of the unity we seek and also as a means for achieving it.'[37] Again: 'Churches which lack the episcopal succession are asked to realise that the continuity with the church of the apostles finds profound expression in the successive laying on of hands by bishops and that, though they may not lack the continuity of the apostolic tradition, this sign will strengthen and deepen that continuity.'[38] *The Report of the Conversations between the Church of England and the Methodist Church* is even more explicit: 'It seems obvious that unity is best expressed in one man as a permanent official representative. This does not necessarily point to papacy, though a permanent primacy of a bishop amongst his fellows is not incompatible with biblical principles, provided no unscriptural claims are made for him' (p. 24).

What all this amounts to is that it is a virtual presupposition of current ecumenical dialogue that episcopacy is to be taken for granted. This is obviously unacceptable to Reformed evangelicals.

1. Virtually no one today claims New Testament sanction for monarchical episcopacy. Even its most ardent exponents claim only that it emerged in the late second century as a logical, Spirit-led development from apostolic times. How can it be claimed that an office which did not even exist in the New Testament is of the essence of the Church?

2. Episcopacy as we know it today contradicts some of the essential principles of New Testament polity: for instance, the plurality of presbyters/bishops in each congregation; and the parity of all presbyters/bishops.

3. There is no evidence that episcopacy has served to maintain either unity or orthodoxy. Its re-imposition in 1666 led, in fact, to the irrevocable break-up of the Church of England; and recent experience shows only too clearly that bishops themselves can be false teachers.

4. Logically, episcopacy is only a midpoint. If we want a focus and a symbol of unity, a Pope is the only final answer.

5. Despite all the protestations that bishops (and popes) are only ministers and servants, it would be foolish to ignore the evidence of history to the contrary. They have too often lorded it over God's heritage.

6. Even in terms of symbolism, they have conveyed to the world a completely wrong image of the Church. Lambeth Palace is not the symbol of service and self-denial but of self-assertion and triumphalism.

To say the least, then, in any discussion on the polity of a future united Church episcopacy could claim no special favours. To hold to it intransigently would simply mean putting up a barrier to all ecumenical advance. We would certainly find it difficult to make the concession made by J. M. Ross (then of the Presbyterian Church of England): 'It is unrealistic to suppose that in England a united church could be other than episcopal, with a ministry in the "Apostolic Succession".'[39]

Church censures

As we have seen, discipline, in the language of the Reformers and their successors, was wider than what we mean by church discipline today. Yet in the narrow sense, referring to the church censures, it was also an important mark of the Church.

The First Book of Discipline (Chapter IX) is typical: 'As no commonwealth can flourish or long endure without good laws and sharp execution of the same, so neither can the kirk of God be brought to purity, neither yet be retained in the same, without the order of ecclesiastical discipline.'

There are three points to be borne in mind.

First, church censures must be directed against sins specifically defined as such by Scripture. The Church's authority is ministerial. We do not make the laws. We merely apply them. To pronounce sinful what Christ has not pronounced sinful is to go beyond our remit and act as tyrants.

Secondly, church censures must be based on clear evidence. The Church must scrupulously avoid infringing natural justice, and rumour and hearsay should count for even less in a 'church court' than they would in a civil one.

Thirdly, it must never be forgotten that Church censures are intended to be restorative, not punitive. They are instruments of pastoral care, aimed at bringing sinners to repentance, not engines of judicial retribution.

Church discipline is probably the weakest area in the modern church and it is fatally easy to turn the apparent absence of this mark into an excuse for leaving the church. We should think very carefully about this, however. Discipline was very lax in the church at Corinth and in the Seven Churches of Asia. Yet neither Paul when writing to the former, nor the Lord when speaking to the latter, ever suggests secession. According to Calvin, our indulgence ought to extend much further in tolerating imperfection of conduct than in tolerating imperfection of doctrine. 'If the holy prophets,' he writes, 'felt no obligation to withdraw from the church on account of the very numerous and heinous crimes, not of one or two individuals, but almost of the whole people, we arrogate too much to ourselves, if we presume forthwith to withdraw from the communion of the church, because the lives of all accord not with our judgment or even with the Christian profession.'[40]

Worship

It is the Westminster Confession which defines worship as one of the marks of the Church: 'Particular churches are more or less pure according as ... public worship is performed as more or less purely in them' (Chap. XXV. IV).

There is one difficulty to be noted in connection with this mark: the distinctive New Testament words for worship (*leiturgeo sebaioō*) are not used in connection with the public gathering of the church. When they are used, they apply to the day-to-day lives of ordinary Christians. This should make us wary of drawing sharp distinctions between the secular and the sacred and between public and private worship. The whole Christian life is an act of worship, in which, as priests, we offer ourselves as sacrifices to God.

On the other hand, the various components of what we commonly regard as worship are associated with the public gatherings of the church. There is glory to God in the church throughout all ages (Eph. 3:21). The gathered church sings psalms and hymns (1 Cor. 14:26). The gathered church prays. The gathered church receives instruction. The gathered church breaks bread.

The New Testament suggests three criteria of worship.

First, is it in the truth? Is it directed to God, biblically conceived, and to Christ as represented in the gospel? The concern here is not merely with orthodoxy but with authenticity. Real worship is in the vertical, designed not to impress a human audience but to please the living God.

Secondly, is it in the Spirit? At one level this is enquiring as to the sincerity, cordiality and spontaneity of our worship. It can so easily become a lifeless form. But there is a deeper challenge, too. Is our worship charismatic, arising out of a real experience of the Spirit's leading and guidance and out of the gifts which He has bestowed upon the congregation?

Thirdly, is the worship conducted decently and in order? If on the one hand there should be no stiff formality, neither, on the other, should there be confusion. The criterion here may very well be the outsider (1 Cor. 14:23). What will he think? Will he think that we are mad?

Distribution

What the Second Book of Discipline calls 'distributions' we today would call the ministry of compassion. The Christian Church was organised for such a ministry from the very beginning, directing its energies towards the sick, the widows and the victims of famine.

Four points deserve to be noticed.

First, the primary beneficiaries under this ministry were the members of the household of faith (Gal. 6:10).

Secondly, believers were also directed to do good to all men (Gal. 6:10).

Thirdly, there was in the early Church (Acts 6:1ff) a group of functionaries (the seven 'deacons') whose specific duty it was to attend to this ministry. They were chosen from among the most gifted members of the community.

Finally, most of what we are told in the New Testament about Christian giving (for example 2 Cor. 8:1ff), relates not to meeting the internal needs of the church but to providing for those who are destitute.

Obviously, this ministry is an essential aspect of the life of the Church. A church which lacks it is radically unfaithful to the New Testament norm.

Perfectionist ecclesiology

The function of these notes or marks of the Church is clearly defined in the Westminster Confession. They are indicators of the relative purity of churches: 'Particular churches are more or less pure according as the doctrine of the gospel is taught and embraced, ordinances administered and public worship performed more or less purely in them' (Chap. XXV.IV).

But in this very same context we have a salutary reminder that 'the purest churches under heaven are subject both to mixture and error'. There are signs among Reformed evangelicals today of a tendency towards a perfectionist ecclesiology. Men act as if it were possible to have a church composed only of true believers and served by elders of only the highest calibre. Men separate in high dudgeon when they discover their churches less than perfect. In actual fact, the choice facing us is not between pure and impure churches, but between churches marked by varying degrees of impurity. All churches are composed of ungodly men who need, individually and collectively, to be justified by grace. 'Sometimes,' said James Durham, 'the Lord in His providence will order so that there is no side can be chosen without inconveniences.' Durham's 'Sometimes' is unnecessary. There are always 'inconveniences', but these must not become an excuse for ignoring the mandatoriness of union between Christians and churches. To quote Durham again: 'By way of precept there is an absolute necessity of uniting laid upon the church, so that it falleth not under debate as a principle whether a church should continue divided or united, more than it falleth under debate whether there should be preaching.' And he adds: We must have union 'with many things defective that need forbearance in persons that are united.'[41]

The situation facing us today is no less confused than it was in Durham's time. Whether we are contemplating joining a local church or leading our churches into wider ecclesiastical union, 'no side can be chosen without inconveniences'. If we have the effrontery to say, 'I am rich and need nothing,' then the Lord will spew us out of His mouth.

Esse and *bene esse*

Reformed theologians have often distinguished between those things which are necessary to the *esse* (being) of a church and those things which are necessary only to its *bene esse* (well-being). James Bannerman is typical: 'There is much that may be necessary to the perfection of a Church that is not necessary to the existence of a Church in such a sense that the want of it would exclude it from the title or privileges of a Church at all.'[42]

This distinction is similar to the one already drawn between primary and secondary doctrines. We cannot use it to distinguish the marks from one another in terms of their relative importance. There is no hierarchy of marks.

With the possible (but improbable) exception of *distributions*, all the marks are essential. The Great Commission itself requires preaching, preachers and baptism. The Church can hardly exist without worshipping: and it has no right to disregard the poor (Gal. 2:10).

The distinction can only operate *within* the marks. Indeed as we have made our way rapidly through the marks, all we have focused on has been the essence: what are *fundamental* doctrines, what is the essence of the sacraments, of polity, of worship and of the ministry of compassion? Within each mark, there are essentials and non-essentials. But each mark is essential.

The important thing now is that Christians who bear the marks (not perfectly but authentically) should recognise, love and serve one another: and that churches which bear the marks (again, not perfectly, but authentically) should, whenever possible, unite: and even where that is not possible, 'stand together, contending with one mind for the faith of the gospel.'

Notes

1. John Calvin, *Institutes* IV.I,2 (London, James Clarke & Co. Ltd., 1962).

2. John Owen, *Works* (London, The Banner of Truth Trust, 1965), Vol. XVI. p.189.

3. Charles Hodge, *The Church and its Polity* (London, 1879) p.89.

4. Howard A. Snyder, *The New Face of Evangelicalism* (London, Hodder and Stoughton, 1976) p.133.

5. John Calvin, *Theological Treatises* (The Library of Christian Classics, Vol. XXII: London, SCM Press, 1954) p.109.

6. Ibid, p.241.

7. Ibid. p.249.

8. John Calvin, *Institutes*, IV.1,12.

9. *The Reformation of the Church*, Ed. Iain H. Murray (London, The Banner of Truth Trust, 1965) p.314.

10. Christopher Butler, *The Theology of Vatican II* (London, Darton, Longman and Todd, 1981), p.125.

11. John Calvin, *Institutes*, IV.I.12.

12. Ibid, IV.II.I.

13. Ibid, IV.I.12.

14. Quoted in James Walker, *Scottish Theology and Theologians* (2nd edition, rpt. Knox Press, Edinburgh, 1982), p.100.

15. John Owen, *Works*, Vol. XVI. p.179.

16. William Cunningham, *Historical Theology* (London, The Banner of Truth Trust, 1960) Vol. II, p.503.

17. Op. cit., Vol. I, p.24.

18. Op. cit., Vol. II, p.184.

19. Op. cit., Vol. II, p.321.

20. Ibid, p.502.

21. William Cunningham, *The Reformers and the Theology of the Reformation* (London, The Banner of Truth Trust, 1967), p.598.

22. George Gillespie, A Treatise of Miscellany Questions (Re-printed in *The Presbyterian's Armoury*, Vol. I: Edinburgh, 1846) Chapter IX.

23. *The Westminster Confession*, Chapter I.VII.

24. John Duncan, *Colloquia Peripatetica* (Edinburgh, 1871), p.59.

25. *The Church and Its Polity*, p.90.

26. John Duncan, *Colloquia Peripatetica,* p.58.

27. Hans Kung, *On Being a Christian* (London, Collins, 1977); Edward Schillebeeckx *Jesus* (London, Collins, 1983).

28. *The Myth of God Incarnate*, Ed. John Hick (London, SCM Press, 1979); Lampe, *God as Spirit* (Oxford, The Clarendon Press, 1977): Mackey, *Jesus: The Man and the Myth* (London, SCM Press, 1979).

29. *All In Each Place: Towards Reunion in England*, Ed. J. I. Packer (Appleford, The Marcham Manor Press, 1965).

30. *The Westminster Confession*, I.VI.

31. *The Canons and Decrees of the Council of Trent*, Twenty-second Session, Chapter II.

32. *The Final Report*, II.5. *The Final Report* is published in *Growth in Agreement* (Geneva, The World Council of Churches, 1984).

33. *The Canons and Decrees of the Council of Trent*, Thirteenth Session, Canon VI.

34. *Growth in Agreement*, p.478.

35. See A. B. Bruce, *The Humiliation of Christ* (Edinburgh, 1876), Lecture III.

36. William Cunningham, *The Reformers and the Theology of the Reformation,* p.240.

37. *Growth in Agreement*, p.485.

38. Ibid, p.496.

39. *All in Each Place*, p.233.

40. *Institutes*, IV.I.18.

41. *The Reformation of the Church*, p.359f.

42. James Bannerman, *The Church of Christ* (London, The Banner of Truth Trust, 1960) Vol. I, p.55f.

Subject Index

Index

From Glory to Golgotha

Controversial Issues in the Life of Christ

Donald Macleod

'Macleod has a unique ability to express complex theological concepts in arresting and thought-provoking language. Not a word is wasted on these pages: as the author explores various aspects of the Person and Work of Jesus Christ, readers will have their minds stretched and their hearts warmed.'

Iain D. Campbell
Back Free Church of Scotland,
Isle of Lewis

'Here is the very heart of Christianity. Here is a "generous orthodoxy", lucidly expounded, honestly defended, and passionately enforced.'

John Nicholls
London City Mission

Here is distilled Macleod: drawn from years of preaching, teaching, and writing, under the most fiery and pressurized of circumstances reduced to its finest, most persuasive essence.'

Duncan Rankin
Reformed Theological Seminary, Jackson, Mississippi

ISBN 1 85792 718 4

A Faith to Live By

Understanding Christian Doctrine

Donald Macleod

A comprehensive examination of Christian Doctrine, practically explained.

'Macleod is a master of making difficult things seem simple, without compromising their profundity ...Macleod is simultaneously an able apologist and a world class exegete (one does not hesitate to mention his name alongside Warfield and Murray in exegetical competence). Read the book. Learn from Macleod. Argue with Macleod. And then bow the knee to your Saviour, the Lord Jesus Christ, and worship!'

**J. Ligon Duncan III,
First Presbyterian Church, Jackson, Mississippi**

'Macleod writes with lucid and sparkling clarity, without sacrifice of detail and definition. Here is excellent theology made both relevant and exciting. I can think of no better book for equipping Christians to present their faith intelligently and attractively to real people.'

John Nicholls, London City Mission

'I have always valued Donald Macleod's writings, his great learning, his respect for those with whom he disagrees, the absence of foolish dogmatism and the presence of a pastoral heart. ...first rate Christian theology'.

Dick Lucas, The Proclamation Trust

ISBN 1 85792 428 2

Shared Life

The Trinity and the Fellowship of God's People

Donald Macleod

'...the simplicity of his style of communication will commend this book to all kinds of folk who currently would have problems in explaining their belief in the Trinity. He commences with proof from Scripture, and adds to this evidence from early Church thinkers before applying Trinitarian religion in a practical way to ourselves... A sound book with the potential to be blessed to many.'

Christian Bookstore Journal

'...gives us a helpful look at the objections raised by Judaism, Islam, Mormonism and the Jehovah Witnesses... extremely helpful. Donald Macleod writes with his customary clarity.'

Evangelism

What is the Trinity?
Why does it matter?
How should it affect us?

'The Doctrine of the Trinity is not simply something to be believed, but something that ought to affect our lives profoundly', say Donald Macleod in this useful book that teaches us about the concept and implications of the doctrine of the Trinty

ISBN 1 85792 128 3

Christian Focus Publications

publishes books for all ages

Our mission statement –

STAYING FAITHFUL

In dependence upon God we seek to help make His infallible word, the Bible, relevant. Our aim is to ensure that the Lord Jesus Christ is presented as the only hope to obtain forgiveness of sin, live a useful life and look forward to heaven with Him.

REACHING OUT

Christ's last command requires us to reach out to our world with His gospel. We seek to help fulfil that by publishing books that point people towards Jesus and help them to develop a Christ-like maturity. We aim to equip all levels of readers for life, work, ministry and mission.

Books in our adult range are published in three imprints.

Christian Focus contains popular works including biographies, commentaries, basic doctrine, and Christian living. Our children's books are also published in this imprint.

Mentor focuses on books written at a level suitable for Bible College and seminary students, pastors, and other serious readers. The imprint includes commentaries, doctrinal studies, examination of current issues, and church history.

Christian Heritage contains classic writings from the past.

For a free catalogue of all our titles, please write to
Christian Focus Publications, Ltd
Geanies House, Fearn,
Ross-shire, IV20 1TW, Scotland, United Kingdom
info@christianfocus.com

For details of our titles visit us on our website
www.christianfocus.com